The School
of Fontainebleau

Etchings and Engravings

Henri Zerner

The School
of Fontainebleau

Etchings and Engravings

Harry N. Abrams, Inc. *Publishers* New York

Translated from the French "L'Ecole de Fontainebleau" by Stanley Baron
Standard Book Number: 8109-0471-3
Library of Congress Catalogue Card Number: 77-95262
All rights reserved. No part of the contents of this book may be
reproduced without the written permission of the publishers
Harry N. Abrams, Incorporated, New York
Copyright 1969 in Great Britain by Thames & Hudson, London
Text printed in Germany
Gravure illustrations printed in France
Bound in Germany

CONTENTS

PREFACE   6

INTRODUCTION   7

    THE PRINTS   13

    THE PRINTMAKERS   17

        FANTUZZI   17

        MASTER L. D.   21

        JEAN MIGNON   26

        ORIGINAL PRINTMAKERS: GEOFFROY DUMOÛTIER,   30
        LÉONARD LIMOSIN, THE SUPPOSED JUSTE DE JUSTE

        THE ENGRAVERS: PIERRE MILAN, DOMENICO DEL BARBIERE   34

PLATES   39

TABLE OF CONCORDANCES   213

INDEX OF PLATES BY SUBJECT   214

SOURCES OF THE PLATES   216

NOTES ON THE PLATES   *Fold out*

TO ANDRÉ CHASTEL

PREFACE

One cannot, indeed, judge books by the effort expended on them. Nevertheless I should like to say that this one is the result of more considerable labour than may appear. The task alone of finding the most satisfactory copies of each work required a great deal of time. The problem of attributions, confronted in many cases, demanded repeated, long sessions, which are summed up in a short phrase. Thus I feel justified in claiming the reader's indulgence for a work whose imperfections will appear only too quickly. For the rest, I am convinced that this book will be useful by virtue of the numerous prints which are reproduced here for the first time, and that the public will take pleasure in looking at these engaging or disquieting images.

Every effort has been made to reproduce a great number of the pieces in their original dimensions, but the reader need not be astonished to find disparities of a few millimeters between the dimensions indicated and the reproduction. The irregularity of the pieces, the difficulty in finding exact markings, and other technical problems explain such divergences. Besides, two proofs from the same plate may have noticeable differences of dimensions.

I would not have been able to manage this work successfully without the assistance of a great many people, particularly collectors and those in charge of public collections. I can mention only a few names: M. Jean Adhémar, Mlles Michèle Hébert and Marie Christine Angebault of the Cabinet des Estampes in the Bibliothèque Nationale; Mme Wanda Bouleau-Rabaud of the Ecole des Beaux-Arts, whose kindness has been unlimited; M. Konrad Oberhuber of the Albertina, Vienna; Mme Marie Mauquoy-Hendrickx of the Bibliothèque Royale, Brussels; Mr Paul Hulton of the British Museum, London; the staff of the Metropolitan Museum, New York; MM. Paul and Hubert Prouté in Paris; and Mr Raymond Lewis in San Francisco.

M. André Chastel, who was kind enough to direct my doctorate thesis, has constantly supported me with both advice and confidence. Mme Sylvie Béguin, whose important works on the School of Fontainebleau are well known, is so closely connected with this book that I have not been able to indicate her innumerable contributions in the course of the text. I also owe several valuable points of information to Mr W. McAllister Johnson. M. Philippe de Montebello has most generously given me access to the documentation he has gathered on Jean Cousin. M. Francis Bouvet kindly read the manuscript and made numerous improvements. Finally I wish to thank my mother, Mme Elisabeth Zerner, and Mr Charles Rosen who have both helped me from the beginning of the work to the reading of proofs.

6

INTRODUCTION

Compared to original, even revolutionary projects like the Châteaux of Chambord or Madrid – products of great architectural efforts – the château built by François I at Fontainebleau was a vast but modest edifice. An exceptionally complete and precise estimate of 1528 shows that, for the sake of economy, as much use as possible was made of the old walls of a ruined medieval castle; a modern appearance was achieved by ornamented dormer-windows and the erection of a monumental entrance, la 'Porte Dorée'.[1] It was clearly the master mason in charge of the work, Gilles Lebreton, who conceived the plans and the decoration. Yet within a few years this mediocre building was to become the artistic centre of France through the activities of the decorators François I brought there.

Recent research stimulated by the growing interest in mannerism has shown that this was an episode of major importance not only for France, but in the whole of European art. It has also been repeatedly stated that prints played an essential part in the diffusion of the School of Fontainebleau. Nevertheless there has been no comprehensive study of these prints since the articles by Félix Herbet around 1900,[2] and very few of them, with the exception of Boyvin's works studied by Levron,[3] have been reproduced.

Our project is to reproduce a large number of these prints and, at the same time, to provide some clarification of their history. In view of the great abundance of documents and problems, we have chosen to limit ourselves, except in a very few cases, to the production at Fontainebleau itself and to the work of a restricted number of printmakers. In this way we shall attempt to form an ensemble as instructive as possible, in order to advance our understanding of the art of Fontainebleau. But before justifying our choice more precisely and embarking on a discussion of the works, we must first briefly review the artistic activity which took place at Fontainebleau.[4]

In 1531, after several disappointments with the greatest artists of his time – particularly Leonardo da Vinci and Andrea del Sarto who both came to France – François I, extraordinarily tenacious in his plan to acclimatize monumental Italian painting to his kingdom, invited a painter of lesser reputation, but young and marvellously gifted: the Florentine Rosso. A year later it was Primaticcio who was invited in his turn, on the recommendation of Giulio Romano, Raphael's official heir, in whom François I had great confidence. Even younger than Rosso and still unknown, Primaticcio was to show the greatest talent; in the course of nearly forty years, he worked assiduously on the decorations of the Château. Each of these two great masters had his international staff of workers and artists, among whom Italians predominated – at least in the important rôles. Brought to a foreign country, in an isolated dwelling, they had to decorate a new and even unfinished building, whose architecture was indifferent and whose

---

[1] Document published by Léon de Laborde, *Les Comptes des Bâtiments du Roi (1528-71)*, Paris 1877, pp. 25-50.

[2] Félix Herbet, 'Les Graveurs de l'Ecole de Fontainebleau', *Annales de la Société archéologique du Gâtinais*. I. 'Catalogue de l'Œuvre de L.D.', 1896, pp. 56-102. II. 'Catalogue de l'Œuvre de Fantuzzi, 1896, pp. 275-91. III. 'Dominique Florentin et les burinistes', 1899, pp. 1-53. IV. 'Les Eaux-fortes nommées ou marquées', 1900, pp. 293-355. V. 'Les Eaux-fortes anonymes', 1902, pp. 55-86 (containing additions and corrections). There are off prints of these numbers with individual pagination.

[3] Jacques Levron, *René Boyvin, graveur angevin du XVIe siècle*, Angers 1941.

[4] The basic work remains L. Dimier, *Le Primatice*, Paris 1900, to which must be added S. Béguin, *L'Ecole de Fontainebleau*, Paris 1960, of which a new edition is anticipated which will bring research up to date.

principal room had proportions which were unpromising and novel for the Italians: very long, narrow and low-ceilinged, the gallery is like an immense corridor.

In such altogether exceptional conditions, these artists were obliged to renovate the decorative repertory of Italian art, and this at a moment when, despite a great many successes, the early Tuscan mannerism was in decline and the great art of Rome had been destroyed by the sack of 1527. Hardly any centres remained but Mantua and Venice, and the examples provided by the latter were too difficult to follow. If one considers the location of Fontainebleau, which was like a geographical link between Italy and Flanders (whose artists were becoming increasingly numerous), one can easily understand how it was able to attract attention and become in some degree the centre of European art.

We still have to consider what is meant by the term School of Fontainebleau, what it implies historically, what defines it stylistically, and to what extent it is critically useful. It has proved to be a convenient term, but at the same time it has been excessively extended to take in all work that was italianized though not actually Italian, whose elongated forms are vaguely reminiscent of the gods and goddesses of Fontainebleau. One finds a great quantity of Flemish painting, the entire School of Prague, and much German painting indiscriminately mingled under the increasingly imprecise label of the School of Fontainebleau.

It is preferable to reserve this term for the art produced at Fontainebleau itself and for that which derives directly from it, such as the Chambre des Arts in the Château of Ancy-le-France, or the decorations of Écouen. The Château of Fontainebleau was the meeting-place for artists of various origin, who had already developed a mature style when they arrived there. Thus in the nineteenth century Rosso and Primaticcio were sometimes violently contrasted, the latter being described as Raphael's artistic grandson, somewhat degenerate but nevertheless heir to the noble classical art, whereas the former was regarded as the frantic exaggerator of Michelangelo's worst excesses and accused of mannerism, with everything most pejorative and indeed shameful that that term has ever implied.

Even among the assistants of these great masters, there were also distinguished artists of various origin who arrived with established reputations. The Florentine Luca Penni supplied a Roman style whose refined heaviness was quite remote from Primaticcio as well as from Rosso. Niccolò dell'Abbate, like the Bolognese Primaticcio a native of Emilia, is outside our frame of reference because the works with which we are concerned were done before his arrival; he was already a mature and very famous artist when he appeared at Fontainebleau. Others whom we know less well, particularly the Flemish, may have introduced other aspects. In spite of these disparities, however, daily collaboration, the effect of the place in which all the artists were crowded together, as it were, and the taste of their patrons gave a certain cohesion to the art of Fontainebleau. And if it has been possible to question the meaning itself of the School of Fontainebleau, the difficulty seems to us of a critical and not an historical order. What this means is that although the phenomenon may be difficult to describe, to analyze and to explain, its historical existence is not in question. In the nineteenth century, the existence of a School of Fontainebleau was felt so strongly by critics that the contributions of Rosso and Primaticcio to the decorations of the Château were ultimately confused. This confusion, as well as the above-mentioned contrast between the two artists, are gross approximations of a complex situation which has come to be customarily and, in the end, conveniently designated by the term School of Fontainebleau.

The changes that took place at Fontainebleau in the style of the artists (at least the best-known) who worked there provide an indirect approach to the cohesion of the movement. Of all the mannerist artists of the early period, Rosso was the most definitely anti-classical. With brutal audacity he was unconditionally opposed, from the outset, to the continuous space and the equilibrium between nature and symmetry which had cost the High Renaissance so much effort. Even after his sojourn in Rome, his art was arbitrary, artificial, almost abstract, and violently expressive. At Fontainebleau his style was transformed. Daily contact with Primaticcio, the more monumental character of the works he had to execute, the necessity of working with numerous assistants, the influence of patrons and the environment certainly played their part; perhaps, up to a point, it was also a natural maturity. Rosso must have felt that the principles behind *Moses Defending Jethro's Daughters* (Uffizi, Florence) could not be developed in the dimensions of a fresco. He may also have been one of those artists who are taught by time to retract their youthful audacities. During his stay at Fontainebleau, he deepened the space in his paintings and modelled his figures with greater relief. Without any loss of vigour, his art became more complex and refined.

But these were nuances and as far as essentials are concerned, Rosso's painting remained what it had been. There is, however, a domain in which the novelties he introduced appeared first at Fontainebleau itself and are more intimately linked with the general work on the project. We are referring, of course, to the ornamentation, the astonishing mixture of painting and stucco which frames the compositions of the Galerie François I and enlivens the room. Though there can be no doubt that the novel decorative system exhibited there was Rosso's work, it may be that he was directly influenced by Primaticcio in his choice of media, and even that Primaticcio had some part in the creation of the work.

Primaticcio, indeed, arrived from Mantua bringing with him the teaching of Giulio Romano. And the only work we know of, through Vasari, that was executed by Primaticcio under his master's direction happens to be a stucco frieze, *The Triumph of Sigismund* (Palazzo del Tè, Mantua). At the very beginning of his activities at Fontainebleau, Primaticcio framed his paintings with stucco ornaments. It is probable that these examples inspired Rosso, and it is not impossible that he asked for Primaticcio's help in a special field of which the latter had particular experience.

Primaticcio, being very young, was even more open to the influence of an older and more illustrious artist, and also doubtless more flexible by temperament as a true spiritual heir of Raphael. We know of almost no works prior to his arrival in France, which in itself suggests that his personality had not yet settled. His first works at Fontainebleau show that he was loyal to his Mantuan training, which was coloured with an Emilian heritage of soft and fluid elegance. He was always to preserve that impression of astonishing luminism of the Sala di Psiche in the Palazzo del Tè, painted precisely during his stay in Mantua. This luminism was totally alien to Rosso. But Primaticcio must soon have been marked by the Florentine in a decisive way. In his figures, the elasticity of the joints, so foreign to Giulio Romano who, on the contrary, stiffened them, certainly came to Primaticcio from Rosso. The canon of his figures borrowed the Michelangelesque element in Rosso: the highly developed torsos of the men, the strong thighs of the women, the physical glorification of humanity.

Primaticcio's journeys to Rome, in 1540 and the following years, put him in contact with the works of antiquity which he collected for the king. But he transformed them by his vision, and when he drew rather coarse Roman figures he brought to them a Greek exquisiteness, as if he wanted to prevent the brilliant world of a legendary antiquity from disappointing the French court. At this point in his career, Primaticcio contributed more to antiquity than he borrowed from it. On the other hand, during his journeys he must have studied with the greatest interest the works of Correggio and, above all,

Parmigianino. Under their influence he defined his characteristic figures more precisely, particularly his women with their strong hips, small and fine faces extended by long necks. At this source he renewed his stock of Emilian sensitivity and sensuality, even before the arrival of Niccolò dell'Abbate, who merely accentuated this development.

During the years before the middle of the century, Luca Penni's personality is strong enough to demand attention when one seeks to relate the stylistic components of the School of Fontainebleau. Brother of Giovanni Francesco Penni, one of Raphael's main assistants, Luca Penni sprang directly from the Roman environment. He worked on the Galerie François I and may well have been attracted to France by Rosso because of his Florentine origin. But those of his works which are known - drawings as well as compositions engraved by various masters - are perhaps no earlier than 1540. We find in them a personality which is distinct and even perhaps a bit rigid, a manner which is sometimes not particularly engaging but always individual. Since one cannot follow his work from its beginnings, it is only through analysis that one can conjecture what he owed to the Fontainebleau circle and what he brought to it. His figures with their frozen gestures, even in violent scenes, show the persistence of his Roman tutelage, but the example of Primaticcio did not leave him untouched. His figures are muscular but lacking in Primaticcio's elasticity. His women have a cold elegance, strong figures, narrow noses, and eyes sunk in deep and elongated sockets. His scenes are bathed in a solemn antique atmosphere. His method of composition without depth may owe something to Rosso. Finally, Penni adopted the ornaments of the Fontainebleau School to his own taste by increasing the weight of the forms and giving more density to the texture of the motifs, which he was gifted at arranging skilfully. The frames of his prints show that he was a master in this field.

We must finally mention Léonard Thiry, the Flemish painter who was one of Rosso's principal assistants. Several of his drawings are known, and a great many others have been reproduced by a number of printmakers. In the well-known group of *L'Histoire de la Toison d'or*, engraved by Boyvin, he appears to be a clever imitator of Rosso, but without great originality. Master L.D. etched from Thiry's designs two collections of a dozen landscapes with figures, one with Pluto and Proserpine, the other with Jupiter and Callisto; these are not reproduced here in their entirety, but one example can be found in Pl. LD 94. In addition, Ducerceau has transmitted to us a group of imaginary views composed of antique ruins. It is in these landscapes that Thiry shows originality. The dates of the prints - 1550 for those by Ducerceau, and probably a similar date for those by L.D. - do not enable us to determine whether it was Thiry who introduced the taste for landscape to Fontainebleau. The fact that he was Flemish makes him a probable candidate for that rôle. One can observe, however, that the landscapes by Fantuzzi, and the very personal ones with which Jean Mignon furnished the backgrounds of his etchings, are quite different from the ones we know to be by Thiry. Whatever the case, this is one of those original and not yet properly understood aspects of the School of Fontainebleau in which Thiry may well have had some influence.

A more complete knowledge of the painting of Fontainebleau would surely confirm the multiplicity of reciprocal influences. We do not believe that these would teach us much about the means by which the environment and the special conditions affected the stylistic crystallization which took place at that time. There is no doubt that a number of less strong personalities would appear distinctly, but one must not exaggerate the advantages of such information, for the works of those unknown artists represent not only a diminution of the style to its least common denominator, but a debasement of its significance.

It is in the domain of ornament that one can best see what happened. Under the differences introduced by each artist, common aspects continued to exist. First of all, an original decorative system defined by the relationship between figures that were at once animated yet always charged with architectonic significance, and linking elements, particularly strap-work[1] but also garlands and the like. These have an essentially architectural rôle but generally are not, properly speaking, architectural elements and therefore preserve a constant liveliness which extends to the whole composition. The various elements are not new. The numerous figures leaning on their elbows, for example, obviously come from Michelangelo; the garlands, even the strap-work, are previously found in Italy. The originality of the Fontainebleau ornamentation lies in the utilization of these elements, in the ambiguity of their function, which causes them all to participate in the structure of the decoration while at the same time they are subject to the general animation. Many examples could be cited among the etchings reproduced here: Pl. AF 40 by Fantuzzi, for instance. Thus one can understand the abundance of the strap-work, which serves as abstract representations of the plane surface but is constantly forced into movement. In a more superficial way, the repetition of characteristic motifs (certain garlands, for example, or certain figures) ultimately gives homogeneity to the decoration of Fontainebleau.

Moreover, it is not a matter only of a visual vocabulary, a world of forms. It is tied up with a repertory of themes – one might call it an iconographic style – which stresses the courtly, erotic and ambiguously sensual character, restless without anguish, of this sophisticated art. The characters of pagan mythology inhabit this world of images with ease; the gods and heroes move freely there in a poetic atmosphere, which Ronsard and the poets of the Pléiade were to make their own – without ever acknowledging their source of inspiration.

The constant reappearance of Achilles, Hercules, Diana, reminds us that the art of Fontainebleau exists to define the image of the living hero. The aim is clear. It was only fitting to celebrate the glory of the king, the beauty of the women, the valour of the heroes of the day, to ornament the life of the court by projecting its events, large and small, on the walls between which it moved. This does not necessarily involved a day-by-day chronicle or a strict correlation between fable and fact. Not that there is an absence of allusion. We know, for instance, that at least a few of the compositions in the Galerie François I refer to episodes in the king's life. But even E. Panofsky's study of the cycle[2] – the most recent, the most complete and also the most convincing – leaves certain doubts. In any case, the difficulty is so great that one must see in it a taste for the obscure. The overuse of familiar themes made one look for unusual subjects, in the way one sought new and surprising motifs. And the subtlety of the allusions does indeed seem to have been a court pastime.

But if an exact deciphering is difficult and often uncertain, it is not really essential. More important, in our opinion, is the general tone of the themes, their reference to favourite aspects of the life at court; compared to an exact deciphering, indeed because of its difficulty, the diffuse suggestion of possible allusions appears to be of the greatest importance. From this arises the popularity of all those fables in which hunting or bathing scenes occur, particularly in a romantic context. We can also understand the constant dialogue between Venus and Diana, between warm and frigid beauty – the latter finally

[1] This term ('cuirs') is used because this ornament looks like a piece of cut leather whose ends roll up.
[2] Dora and Erwin Panofsky, 'The Iconography of the Galerie François Ier at Fontainebleau', *Gazette des Beaux Arts*, September 1958.

triumphant (but only after the period of our prints) when it crystallized around the dominating personality of Diane de Poitiers. From 1540, even before the advent of Henri and Diane, a Fontainebleau Paris would not have given the apple to Venus without hesitation. It is a question of a taste and an ideal of love which permeated an epoch.

State politics and the glory of the patron also had their place. In this context one will notice a marked preference for Greek over Roman subjects. Such a predilection has a double justification. One is stylistic: the elegant art of Fontainebleau was more suited to the Greek legends than to the violent episodes of Roman history. But here there is certainly a political aspect, for the Roman themes were almost inevitably identified with themes of empire, whereas the Greek ones, particularly that of Alexander the Great, were royal themes and welcome to the court. One feels constantly behind these choices the shadow of the conflict with the Emperor Charles V, which was the main preoccupation of François I's reign.

It is understandable that sacred art remains somewhat peripheral. Not that it is absent or lacking in interest; many examples in our collection prove the contrary. The piety and mysticism of a period during which religious problems became increasingly acute, were perfectly adapted to the sophistications of Fontainebleau's art, and once again Diane de Poitiers was to provide the most accomplished model. But religious problems were not determining factors in artistic invention.

In all of its important and original aspects, the School of Fontainebleau is directly linked with the creation of a décor for living. The conditions were not altogether different from those at Mantua. But Giulio Romano never freed himself from the solemnity of the environment of his youth in which the great Vatican projects determined the dominant style: the Sistine Chapel, the Stanze, the Sala di Costantine. The pomp and majesty of those places demanded a permanent and universal style. At Mantua, Giulio always retained something of that loftiness of tone which, technically speaking, requires a certain separation between the expressive and decorative aspects of art, between the ornament and the subject, to make possible the intensity of expression. It is precisely the fusion – or better, the peculiar equilibrium – of these two functions of art, of decoration and expressive image, which accounts for the originality of the art of Fontainebleau. For if, as has been said, the ornaments are remarkably lively and expressive, the subject compositions, for their part, have highly developed decorative and abstract qualities. The spectacular lesson of the Galerie François I was not to be forgotten, even when Rosso's particular style was in eclipse.

Moreover, this fusion, this intermediary condition of art, affected not only the forms; it can be seen in the iconography. Despite the playful way the themes are treated, the mythology and legend represented are not yet relegated to that merely decorative rôle in which they were to be imprisoned in the following centuries. The gods and heroes of Fontainebleau are more than the enciphered description of contemporary society, more than a gallant metaphor. Without the conviction of the fifteenth century, without the intellectual vigour of the High Renaissance, the artists of Fontainebleau still charged their representations with a degree of 'demonic' energy, glorification of the characters through the physical poetry of the figures.

The relation mentioned above between the decoration and the pictorial expression largely determines the meaning and the possibilities of this art. One limitation appears immediately: the sublime is excluded. But there are gains in other directions. Thus, few types of art have been capable of such a rich eroticism; the licentious extravagance of the pictures is, so to speak, shielded by the decorative significance, always richly charged with motifs. Since the attention is at once captured by the dynamism of the forms, it is only through examination that the mind deciphers them. For example, the unambiguous action of the central subject in *Femmes au bain* (Pl. JM 46), by Mignon after Penni, emerges only after the formal poetry has established a climate which makes the subject acceptable.

Above all it is necessary to think of the School of Fontainebleau as a complete manifestation in the whole of its production and without dividing the themes from the forms. This is the only way to appreciate the character of this décor which places us on an unstable and ambiguous level of consciousness where, under cover of a humour which guarantees spiritual health, any audacity is permitted.

THE PRINTS

It is precisely with relation to prints that the term School of Fontainebleau was originally used. Adam Bartsch, the great Viennese iconophile, appears to have been the first to use it in his vast catalogue, *Le Peintre-Graveur*.[1] He applied the name School of Fontainebleau to a group of prints, most of them etchings and a good many of them anonymous, having common characteristics which made them a fairly homogeneous ensemble. 'All these prints,' he wrote, 'are generally etched in somewhat the same taste and in a free manner which leaves no doubt that they were the work of painters.'[2]

He placed this group at the end of his sixteenth volume devoted to Italian etching, the free etching of which Parmigianino had given the first examples, and of which the Fontainebleau etchings are the direct extension. Since then, the term School of Fontainebleau has continued to be used in the history of printmaking, while new names were added to the list, particularly René Boyvin, whose numerous engraved plates are in fact based above all on the designs of Fontainebleau artists: Rosso, Luca Penni, Léonard Thiry. Even Ducerceau, Etienne Delaune and Dupérac have been annexed to the School.

The term was expanded in this way by Félix Herbet, whose basic work, published in a regional scholarly review, is unfortunately not easily accessible and has no illustrations. Herbet was a historian not of prints but of Fontainebleau. He applied himself to the description of the prints because they constitute an essential documentation in the study of the Château's decoration. He also included artists like Giorgio Ghisi, who were entirely outside the School but made prints of certain works by the Fontainebleau artists. Herbet's point of view also explains why it was fundamentally of little importance to him whether a plate was executed by one artist rather than another. Though his catalogues are remarkably complete, his attributions are not always convincing.

Jules Lieure, best known for his monumental work on Callot, was, on the contrary, a historian of prints. He felt the need to take up the whole question again from this perspective by reverting to the more restricted conception of Bartsch, developed by Renouvier. One can see this in his excellent short manual, 'L'École française de gravure des origines à la fin du XVIe siècle'.[3] It is most regrettable that he was unable to complete his studies of the printmakers of the School of Fontainebleau, and particularly the catalogue which he was preparing on Jean Mignon.[4]

The present collection places itself, in some degree, in the line of Bartsch and Lieure in an attempt to circumscribe the problem. Three things must be distinguished: the etchings whose unity Bartsch

---

[1] Adam Bartsch, *Le Peintre-Graveur*, v. 16, Vienna 1818. [2] *Ibid*, p. 300.

[3] Jules Lieure, *L'Ecole française de gravure des origines à la fin du XVIe siècle*, Paris n.d. (1928).

[4] Lieure's notes are in the Cabinet des Estampes of the Bibliothèque Nationale, where we have been able to consult them.

apprehended; a group of engravings whose appearance is homogeneous enough for one to have attributed them *en bloc* to René Boyvin, though one knows now, as will be shown later, that he was not their sole author; and finally, isolated prints which reproduce works of the Fontainebleau artists, executed by Delaune, Philippe Galle, Bonasone. These last are often of great interest but need not concern us here. In their style and presentation, the engravings of the Boyvin group and the etchings in fact form two distinct groups, united only because they are both reflections of Fontainebleau art. Furthermore, the engravings, executed in Paris over a long period beginning about 1540, manifest a certain break with what was actually taking place at Fontainebleau in their total neglect of the work of Primaticcio and their fidelity to Rosso. This in no way excludes certain contacts, and that is why we have deemed it necessary to raise, at least summarily, the problem of the engravings and to introduce Boyvin's predecessor, the engraver Pierre Milan. But it is the etchings which are of primary interest, for they constitute, properly speaking, the School of Fontainebleau in prints.

A good many pieces have to be added to the *corpus* drawn up by Bartsch. It is a matter of sheets which he did not know about, or of the works of printmakers like Dumoûtier or Léonard Limosin which he excluded because their being French set them outside his project. Thus one arrives at about 500 or 600 sheets. Among this mass of documents, most of which bear no mark at all, one can distinguish several print-makers' hands; and successive writers, especially Renouvier[1] and Herbet, have facilitated great progress in the identification and allotment of these prints. Three principal masters stand out: Master L.D. (called Léon Daven), Fantuzzi and Jean Mignon, whose works form the basis of this collection. Another print-maker marked a certain number of pieces with the monogram 1.♀.V. His style changes greatly from one piece to another, and it seems probable that some of the anonymous etchings are by him. We have excluded him not only because his contribution is difficult to determine, but also because he is a much more uneven artist than the others.

The period during which the etchings were made can be established with some precision. If the dated pieces are not numerous, the dates they bear are eloquent: the earliest is 1542, the latest 1548; 1543 and 1544 are the most frequent. As we shall see later in discussing the individual printmakers, there are good reasons for thinking that the years 1542 and 1548 are more or less the extreme dates of this production. On the other hand, the physical resemblances among the prints permit us to conjecture that they were executed in one place. Fantuzzi, the most productive etcher of the school, was during these very years one of Primaticcio's principal assistants in the decoration of the château. It is, therefore, almost certain that these etchings were made at Fontainebleau itself. One must consequently assume that a workshop for prints was installed at Fontainebleau and functioned for approximately six years, from 1542 to 1547 or 1548. Confirmation may be found in the fact that none of the numerous decorations of the château reproduced by these etchers is later than 1545.

As far as we can judge, the printmakers of Fontainebleau worked from drawings and not from paintings. Among such a great number of etchings, it is striking to find none, with one exception, which reproduce the famous masterpieces of Leonardo da Vinci, Raphael and Andrea del Sarto, which were the glory of François I's collections and which were actually displayed at Fontainebleau. In fact the printmakers' repertory is almost exclusively limited to five names: Rosso, Primaticcio, Giulio Romano,

---

[1] Jules Renouvier, *Des types et des manières des maîtres graveurs*, Montpellier 1853-55.

14

Parmigianino and Luca Penni. Giulio Romano, as we have seen, was Primaticcio's master and there can hardly be any doubt that the drawings by Giulio at Fontainebleau belonged to his pupil. This is probably true also of the drawings by Parmigianino. Primaticcio's admiration for this artist is apparent, and it was more marked after 1540. It is also probable that Primaticcio collected some of his drawings during trips to Italy in 1540 and a little later. As for the drawings by Rosso, it seems probable that they too passed to Primaticcio after his death. It is known that Rosso died without an heir and that his property, which was considerable, therefore accrued to the king. The latter probably did not care about the drawings; since Primaticcio succeeded Rosso as general director of the Fontainebleau decorations, it is likely that he likewise inherited Rosso's studio. If this is accepted, it would signify that the drawings etched at Fontainebleau, with the exception of Luca Penni's, were more or less all in Primaticcio's hands. He therefore had the capacity to control the reproduction, to encourage it or bring it to a halt. For this reason, and in a more general way because of the great authority he exercised, one can assume that Primaticcio had a personal part in the vogue for etching at Fontainebleau, and perhaps also in its abrupt disappearance. Indeed it is not impossible that the great painter did some etching himself. Tradition attributes to him one sheet, whose manner appears in no other and whose style is close enough to his to make such an attribution not impossible. Thus Primaticcio may have executed a single etching, as Rubens did. But his contribution to the prints of Fontainebleau is far greater than this isolated attempt.

It is likely that Luca Penni, who was on the spot, played an independent rôle. Vasari's reference to him should be enough to convince us of this and to demonstrate his importance, but Vasari's information is confused and, in part, certainly false. On one hand he implies that Penni himself made prints, but elsewhere he speaks only of Penni's furnishing designs for the etchers.[1] The recent suggestion that the monogram L.D. should be read as Luca Delineavit and that the works of this master should be attributed to Penni[2] is not plausible. Aside from the fact that such a form would be without precedent, the character of these works prohibits such an attribution. While we cannot affirm that Penni never made prints, we do not know where we are supposed to look for his hand. On the other hand, his place in the print-making of Fontainebleau is important because of the many compositions he provided for the etchers. One of them, identified as Jean Mignon, devoted himself almost entirely to reproducing Penni's designs. There are also a good number in the work of Master L.D. As far as can be judged, it seems that designs by Penni became more numerous in Master L.D.'s work around 1547, at the same time that designs by Primaticcio became less frequent. One might say that around this period, when printmaking was declining at Fontainebleau, it drew its inspiration from Penni. Later, when the Fontainebleau etchers ceased production, Penni's designs continued to be reproduced elsewhere. René Boyvin, who engraved nothing of Primaticcio's but went on imperturbably reproducing the inventions of Rosso, executed a number of designs by Penni. Besides, the two men were in direct contact since, shortly before his death, Luca apprenticed his son Lorenzo to Boyvin, a proof of his trust in the man and interest in his profession.[3] At least occasionally, Penni was also his own publisher, as is proved by the inventory

[1] Giorgio Vasari, *Le Vite*, ed. Milanesi, v. 4 (Florence 1879), in which Vasari speaks only of drawings given to the printmakers; and v. 5 (Florence 1880), p. 434, a passage that is confused and difficult to interpret, in which Vasari seems to indicate that Penni made prints, but speaks of wood-engravings, perhaps in error.

[2] Paul Vanaise, 'Nouvelles précisions concernant la biographie et l'œuvre de Luca Penni', *Gazette des Beaux Arts*, LXVII, 1966, pp. 79-89.

[3] Pierre du Colombier, 'Le graveur Laurent Penni', *Humanisme et Renaissance*, III, 1936, pp. 327-29.

after his death; in this are mentioned the copperplates of a series of *Capital Sins*, which will be discussed below in connection with Master L.D.[1] Penni certainly earned a part of his income from prints and one often has the impression that his drawings were intended for printmaking.

These observations lead us to believe that one must distinguish two things in the prints of Fontainebleau: on one hand, the graphic work after Penni, which was pursued at Paris; and on the other, the ensemble of etchings after Rosso, Primaticcio, Giulio Romano and Parmigianino, whose inspiration seems to us to emanate from Primaticcio, and whose most perfect representative is Fantuzzi, who, it may be remarked, did no etchings from designs by Penni.

The study of prints which reflect the art of Fontainebleau confirms the deep division between the group of etchings and the engravings executed at Paris. It is not a matter simply of differences of technique and presentation. The work of the engravers is more exclusively decorative; even when it is a question of interpreting the large historical compositions, the system of hatching is so methodical, the arabesque so insistent, the cut of the burin in the copper so strongly marked, that the representation loses some of its significance to the graphic effect itself. Also, these engravers are most successful in the field of ornament. Somewhat marginal and soon out of date, their work is the patient, commercial, almost artisan-like exploitation of the art of Fontainebleau.

The etchings, on the other hand, are more faithful to the Fontainebleau spirit, which we have attempted to define earlier. But at the same time, their intention is more difficult to grasp. In other words, why have all these plates been etched? They often have a non-commercial character. Whereas the engravings of Pierre Milan were printed in great number, as shown by the documents as well as the fact that plates were worn out and restored, the etchings, because of their technique itself, allowed only for smaller editions. What is more, the plates were evidently not exploited to the full: a plate by L.D., for example, was still in excellent condition in the seventeenth century when François Langlois published a new edition. Many of the plates are so badly etched that prints from them were surely very few indeed and, in any case, not very saleable.

To say that it was a fad is not sufficient explanation, even if it were true. We believe that it must be viewed as a manifestation of self-awareness. That massive publication, so enthusiastic and so transitory, took place at precisely the moment when what we understand as the School of Fontainebleau crystallized. It was also the exact period when the decorations of the Galerie François I were reproduced in tapestry. That was a monumental and, apparently, unprecedented act of homage to the departed genius of Rosso.[2] In the choice of artists whose compositions were engraved, there seems to have been a deliberate plan: everything, with very few exceptions, has a direct bearing on the stylistic crystallization which occurs around Primaticcio after the death of Rosso. Particularly the prints which we can date from 1542 to 1544 give the impression of a virtual manifesto. The numerous dates one finds on the sheets of these years stress this impression of a consciousness of history. One might say that the artists, Primaticcio foremost, understood the importance of their activities; their accomplishment greatly exceeded the limits of the isolated residence of Fontainebleau, and it was necessary to make this public, with whatever means were at hand. The immediate success of their production proved them right. As for us, we are most grateful to them for this faithful news report of a great artistic moment.

[1] See note 2, p. 15.

[2] This unfinished tapestry is in the Kunsthistorisches Museum, Vienna. See Kurt Kusenberg, *Le Rosso*, Paris 1931, pp. 120–21.

THE PRINTMAKERS

Some words of explanation are required to justify the selection of printmakers whose work is reproduced here. The three most important etchers appear: Fantuzzi, Master L.D., and the supposed Jean Mignon. The volume could have been completed with the remaining prints which come closest to theirs, i.e., those of Master I. ♀. V. and those which are anonymous or bear isolated monograms. We have preferred to eliminate these works, which are generally more mediocre, and to introduce, on one hand, original etchers (those who executed their own inventions): Geoffroy Dumoûtier, Léonard Limosin and the supposed Juste de Juste; and, on the other hand, two engravers, Domenico del Barbiere and Pierre Milan. The admirable works of Domenico find a place here naturally since he is one of the important artists who worked at Fontainebleau during the period that concerns us. As for Milan, he was engraving in Paris at exactly the same time that our etchings were being executed at Fontainebleau, and after the same masters. It appears to have been he who established what may be called the School of Paris engravers. As a result, he offers a valuable point of comparison. Moreover, certain affinities between his manner and that of Domenico del Barbiere or that of the few burin engravings by L.D. make the confrontation desirable, even though it is not easy to define the exact relationship among these masters. Milan's work, however, is so difficult to separate from that of Boyvin that it has seemed preferable in this case to adhere to the documented engravings that can be definitely identified rather than to attempt to form a catalogue. Boyvin worked mainly after 1550, and his voluminous output neither can nor should be included. In short, we have sought to show the essential in what was etched at Fontainebleau between about 1540 and 1550, with enough examples of works done in Paris to permit a comparison.

FANTUZZI

Of all the Fontainebleau etchers, Fantuzzi is the one about whom we have the most information, though that is not much. He is also the one whose work has the clearest profile. We will not hark back here to an old confusion which identifies our Antonio Fantuzzi with an engraver of chiaroscuro wood-cuts, Antonio da Trento, whose relations with Parmigianino are reported by Vasari.[1] Nothing is known about Fantuzzi outside of his stay at Fontainebleau, and all that is known of that comes from the Château accounts (in which he is mentioned twice) and from indications which can be drawn from the prints themselves. From 1537 to 1540 he was paid at the rate of 7 *livres* a month to work under Primaticcio on the decoration of the room (of which there is no longer any trace) above the Porte Dorée. Seven *livres* was the smallest salary received by any artist at Fontainebleau, which means that Fantuzzi must have been an assistant of little importance. But in the general settlement from 1541 to 1550 we find him in far better circumstances. 'A Anthoine Fantoze, paintre, pour ouvrages de paintures qu'il a faits et pour avoir vacqué aux patrons et pourtraits en façon de grottesque pour servir aux autres paintres besognans aux ouvrages de painture de la grande gallerie estant en la basse court dudit chasteau, à raison de vingt liv. par mois.' At 20 *livres*, Fantuzzi now had the highest salary of any of Primaticcio's assistants until the arrival of Niccolò dell'Abbate. Also, the note concerning him is one of the most complete. The work

---

[1] A discussion of this subject will be found in Henri Zerner, 'L'eau-forte à Fontainebleau - Le rôle de Fantuzzi', *Art de France*, IV, 1964, pp. 70-85. The artist signed Fantuzi with only one z, but it seems to us more convenient to use the normal orthography which is found everywhere else.

in question is Primaticcio's most important one, the Galerie d'Ulysse, a universally admired master-piece unfortunately destroyed in the eighteenth century. This gallery, extremely long and narrow, was decorated with a multitude of compositions set in a system of ornamental arabesques called 'grotes-ques', harking back to the Vatican Loggie decorated under Raphael's direction. The important rôle played by the ornamentation vouches for Fantuzzi's considerable contribution, since he was charged not only with the execution of paintings but also with the invention of part of the 'grotesques'. From this evidence it seems likely that Fantuzzi made himself a kind of specialist in this field; we shall see that his prints confirm this.

One may be surprised by the sudden change in Fantuzzi's position. It may be explained, however, if one considers at what moment the change took place. At the end of 1540, when Primaticcio was in Rome with the mission of buying antiques and taking casts of famous works, such as the Laocoön and the statue of Marcus Aurelius, Rosso suddenly died, probably a suicide. Primaticcio returned precipi-tately to find himself in charge of the decoration of the Château. He inaugurated an artistic reign which was to last thirty years. A replacement of personnel took place, like a minor revolution, which has been well described by Dimier, Primaticcio's biographer.[1] Bolognese compatriots of Primaticcio took prece-dence over the Florentines introduced by Rosso. That Fantuzzi came from Bologna we know both from the accounts and from the inscription on one of the prints. It may be that he was very young when he came to Fontainebleau and that his first years there were in the nature of an apprenticeship under Primaticcio. This situation explains his abrupt advancement.

None of Fantuzzi's paintings remain, but more than 100 etchings, some signed with his complete name or various monograms and others with no mark at all, inform us about his artistic personality. Aside from sheets of ornamentation, some of which may be his own inventions, and landscapes which he inserted into Rosso's frames, he was generally contented to etch the designs of others. He seems to have been easily influenced by the works he interpreted. But he was a decisive and keen draughtsman, who tended to accentuate the excesses of his models, whether the violence of Giulio Romano or Rosso, or the 'morbidezza' of Primaticcio. If his drawing is sometimes faulty it is never unintelligent, and whereas he is superb when he succeeds, he is at least curious in his bad moments.

Fantuzzi restricted himself to etching, with only a few exceptions. His touch is direct and decided, and in spite of transformations in his style he retains a personal method of drawing, of stressing the con-tour and of indicating the direction of the glance, which makes it possible to attribute to him unhesitating-ly a good number of unsigned pieces, and to reduce the doubtful attributions to very few. In addition, one can determine with some precision the very short period during which he executed all his etchings. The dated sheets are not very numerous but sufficient to mark out several years of graphic activity. One finds that all the dates are between 1542 and 1545. Since the three pieces of 1542 and those which are close to that year show an obvious technical inexperience, it can be assumed that they are among his first etchings. On the other hand, one can assemble only a few pieces in the style of 1544-45, which makes it probable that Fantuzzi slowed down his graphic production and ceased making prints alto-gether in 1545 or a little after.

In the course of these few years we can see a development taking place in Fantuzzi's style, and at the same time a change in his choice of models. In 1542 he was etching after Giulio Romano above all. Some

---

[1] L. Dimier, *op. cit.*, pp. 69-70.

pieces, like the *Cavaliers suivant une aigle* (Pl. AF 2) – a dated work – have a defective technique. This badly etched plate shows inexpert retouching with the burin; this is true also of the *Satyre violentant une femme* (Pl. AF 19). But Fantuzzi soon learns to treat his plates boldly and to let the acid bite them deeply. Thus he obtains violent luminous effects which are appropriate to the 'barbaresque' character of Giulio Romano's designs, which Fantuzzi handles with surprising understanding. To this period must be dated – aside from the *Clémence de Scipion* (Pl. AF 1) and the series of friezes from the Palazzo del Tè (Pls AF 2–9) – *Une Bataille* (Pl. AF 15), *Prisonniers soumis à des supplices* (Pl. AF 12), the *Combat de Gladiateurs* (Pl. AF 13) and *Régulus dans son tonneau* (Pl. AF 14). No doubt etchings of certain compositions by other masters than Giulio Romano must be added to the same period: compositions by Rosso, such as *Vertumne et Pomone* (Pl. AF 38) or *Pandore* (Pl. AF 22); probably *Circé* (Pl. AF 18), after Parmigianino; at least one subject by Primaticcio, *Hercule se laissant habiller en femme* (Pl. AF 17). Particularly in this last sheet one notices how much Fantuzzi was influenced by his study of Giulio. Primaticcio's design is completely transformed in this direction. Probably we must also add to the same period Fantuzzi's first sheets of ornamentation, e.g. the *Plafond* (Pl. AF 40) or the *Encadrement de la Destruction de Catane* (Pl. AF 34).

The first pieces dated 1543 are still very similar to those of 1542 – for example, *Silène porté par deux bacchants* (Pl. AF 56), which may have been etched after Giulio Romano. During this year the style changes. The touch becomes finer, the texture more compact, the etching more delicate. The graphic system, i.e., the organization of hatching, becomes more complex. The result of this is a lessening of effect, and the plates of this period are not always so successful as those which precede them. Nevertheless there are admirable pieces: it was at this time that Fantuzzi must have etched most of the subjects of the Galerie François I, paintings and ornaments after Rosso. He was still making prints after Giulio Romano, particularly the *Continence de Scipion* (Pl. AF 58) and a large scene of the *Banquet de Scipion* (Pl. AF 57). The *Bain des nymphes* (Pl. AF 59), after Parmigianino, shows that Fantuzzi was now as much influenced by Rosso as by Giulio. It was also in 1543 that he began a series of etchings of antique statues: the two sheets bearing this date are among the most faltering of this group, and the change in style indicates that their execution must have been prolonged into 1544 and perhaps even 1545. These plates were difficult to catalogue because, in the absence of reproductions, they require extremely precise descriptions in order to be distinguished from one another; besides, some of them are exceedingly rare. We are convinced that we have not recovered all the pieces though we reproduce here a greater number than Herbet describes. Several of them bear Roman numerals, so that, at least at one time, there must have been a numbered series. However, we have not been able to reconstitute it, and in any case these numbered pieces vary in style and even in dimensions. These sheets are of great interest, not only because they are very beautiful etchings, but because they surely preserve the memory of drawings after the antique which Primaticcio brought back from his trip to Rome. Today we can form some idea of what Primaticcio contributed to his models, since the discovery by P. Massar[1] of the prototypes of two Fantuzzi prints of a Roman sarcophagus. The immense difference which separates the designs etched by Fantuzzi and the mediocre sculpture that inspired them, the exquisite Atticism of these draped figures, makes one believe that Primaticcio was the intermediary of genius who effected the metamorphosis.[2]

[1] Phyllis Massar, 'The source of a rare Fontainebleau etching', *Art Bulletin*, December 1965, pp. 506–07.
[2] We cannot agree with Mrs Massar that Fantuzzi executed these etchings directly from the antique. F. Zava Boccazzi,

There is only one piece dated 1544, *Saturne endormi* (Pl. AF 72), but it shows that Fantuzzi's style had perceptibly changed in the direction foreshadowed in 1543. This development is accentuated in the three pieces dated 1545. In this period, during which it is difficult to make internal distinctions, the etcher's style becomes freer again and the texture is more open. But from his acquired experience he preserved the methodically placed and varied hatching. For light shadows he made abundant use of stipple. In a general way, the plates are lighter, luminous without the violent contrasts of the first prints. Most of them are more carefully etched. The drawing is also less impetuous and the artist's taste has changed considerably. He etches several designs by Primaticcio and is increasingly influenced by that master; thus it is in a Primaticcian sense that he interprets the designs he etches, such as the *Sainte Famille* (Pl. AF 74) after Rosso or the *Apollon et Marsyas* (Pl. AF 76) after Parmigianino. The same tendency is noticeable in the plates of ornaments which deviate from Rosso's style. It is not impossible that these elegant ornaments, skilfully put together, more symmetrical and calmer than those of 1542-43, were designed by Fantuzzi himself; these would be the only works which enable us to form an idea of an ornamental invention well above the mediocre.

In 1545, Fantuzzi's style seems to become systematized. In the *Chute de Phaéton* (Pl. AF 83) one can see a certain softness derived from an excessive care in the handling of transitions. But the works of this character are very rare, and Fantuzzi appears to have abandoned printmaking at that moment for reasons which are unknown to us.

It is difficult to assess Fantuzzi's capabilities of invention. Most of his prints reproduce designs by other masters, and even among those ornaments whose models are unknown, one cannot be sure which ones he created himself. But there is one innovation that appears to be his, the idea of introducing landscapes in the middle of his etched cartouches. We know that the most important of these did not contain such landscapes originally, since they were the ornamental frames of historical subjects for the Galerie François I; Fantuzzi also etched a certain number of these compositions separately. Two questions arise. Why did Fantuzzi not etch the historical subject within its corresponding ornament? And why did he introduce a landscape in its place? The first can be answered fairly easily. The plates Fantuzzi used for the large ornaments are about 50 cm. long, which must have been the largest format at his disposal. This leaves a length of about 15 to 20 cm. for the interior of the cartouche. With his expansive, free manner Fantuzzi must have found this space too restricted for the complex compositions of Rosso. The type of ornament he reproduced was new in printmaking and the centre of the cartouche had to be filled. It is true that we find some which are left empty, but these are either ornaments with a very small cartouche, or pieces executed some years later, at a time when the success of these etched ornaments permitted this sort of audacity. What gave Fantuzzi the idea of filling these spaces with landscapes rather than figures, for example? Does this correspond to a type of mural decoration? There is no evidence to support this. Though the landscapes seem to be introduced primarily to 'furnish' the

Antonio da Trento incisore (Trento 1962), believed this because she read the date 1540 on one, which would not allow time for Primaticcio to have brought his models back from Rome – but the date is 1543. Nor need one be troubled by the indication *Roma*, which does not apply to the place where the print was executed but to the location of the original. W. McAllister Johnson has drawn my attention to Primaticcio's drawings of antiques noted by Dimier in the Chennevières collection and which have unfortunately disappeared; but marginal sketches in the author's copy deposited in the Cabinet des Estampes permit us to see that one of the drawings was the model for the etching of *Hygie*. This appears to us to confirm Primaticcio's intervention definitively. (Dimier, *Le Primatice*, 1900, p. 469.)

cartouche, perhaps Fantuzzi had an inclination towards this kind of subject. His landscapes are rather personal and, although of a Flemish type, they do not resemble what we know of Thiry's work. Finally it is necessary to point out a general affinity between landscape and ornament; tapestry, at least, offers some early examples of this, and it is also indicated by the great development of this *genre* in mural decoration after the middle of the sixteenth century. These remarks are not intended to diminish the originality of Fantuzzi's ornamental sheets, which established a new kind of print with an admirable posterity. On the contrary, we would suggest that, in this particular case, Fantuzzi inspired monumental decoration more than he imitated it.

Fantuzzi's prints, violent and negligently executed, speak for an exceptionally concentrated artistic culture in a period which has often been represented as wholly devoted to an exhausted eclecticism. At the same time, the rapid variations of the artist's interests and style are revelations of a pioneering artistic environment, in which topicality and excellence are virtually synonymous. Fantuzzi is the model printmaker of the School of Fontainebleau, and it is in relation to him and his work that one can best situate the other artists.

MASTER L.D.

Master L.D. is the finest Fontainebleau etcher. He interpreted Primaticcio's work with a sympathy and taste which have led to comparisons between this collaboration and the one between Marcantonio and Raphael. This praise is not wholly exaggerated. Unfortunately we have much less information on the supposed Daven than on Marcantonio. His personality remains a mystery, and his name itself an enigma. This master of printmaking signed his plates with the monogram L.D., which has been interpreted in different ways. The most widespread view of the last century was that it stood for Léonard Thiry (based on the Flemish form Dirk), but Herbet has treated this dubious identification as it deserves. A recent proposal has been to read *Luca Delineavit* in the monogram, but this hardly stands up to examination.[1] The most probable hypothesis remains the oldest one: Léon Daven (or Davent). It is founded on an inscription at the bottom of a large composition, *Les Apôtres contemplant le Christ et la Vierge* (Pls LD 53–56), etched after Giulio Romano on four large plates. Each plate is marked with the monogram, but in addition one can read at the bottom, astride two plates, the inscription 'Lion daven' and the date 1546 at the extreme right. We are obliged to give this inscription a meaning. Some have seen in Lion the place of publication rather than a name, but this is unsatisfactory because in that case one would read 'à Lion', and besides what does one make of 'daven'?[2] It is still most plausible to read *Lion daven* as the name of the etcher since the initials correspond to the monogram. One cannot object that the initials already appear, for there are plenty of examples of prints that are signed both with initials and the complete name. It is true that 'daven(t)' could also be an appellation of origin rather than a patronym (like the D of the monogram), but it is not a form found elsewhere. Thus we believe that the artist was called Léon Daven. The 't' at the end is a doubtful reading: it is difficult to say whether it is really a letter or a small stroke made by a slip. We adopt the spelling Daven because it is the one given by the first writer, Marolles, who does not say how he knows the name, and who, at a distance of only a hundred years, might have inherited a tradition independent of the inscription in question.

[1] P. Vanaise, *op. cit.*
[2] Those who hold the Thiry theory read 'daventerensis' as the place of the artist's origin, but we have said that Thiry is out of the question; besides, it is not known that Thiry came from Deventer.

The disadvantage of the name Léon Daven is that it remains a dead letter. No author speaks of it, no document mentions it, one cannot attach it to anything but the prints which bear its monogram. Until some discovery takes place to reveal its identity, there is no difference between the name of Master L.D. and Léon Daven, nor any greater convenience in the latter; that is why we continue to use Master L.D., which remains the safest.

The work of L.D. reproduced here is much reduced as compared with Herbet's catalogue, for the following reasons. Herbet's catalogue consists of three parts. The first 95 numbers are pieces that are generally of rather important dimensions in which figures largely dominate; some are engraved and some etched, and the style varies greatly, even if one sets aside certain dubious attributions, to which we shall return. Numbers 96 to 156 correspond to 61 plates of Oriental costumes which illustrate a book entitled *Les quatres premiers livres des Navigations orientales de N. de Nicolay*, published in 1568 by Guillaume Rouille. All these plates are etchings in a monotonous style and almost all are marked L.D. in very small, almost hidden, letters. Finally, numbers 157 to 221 are landscapes with figures; among these, two series of twelve prints each, representing respectively the love of Pluto and Proserpine, and the story of Callisto, are from designs by Léonard Thiry; the rest are etched in a similar style but without the name of the designer.[1] Most of these landscapes are etched in the same, rather drab way and bear the very small monogram L.D., often hidden. The style of these small landscapes and that of the *Navigations orientales* are closely related, and the two sets form a solid whole.

Thus we have two groups of prints bearing the same monogram but of such differing character that it is difficult to reconcile them as the work of the same artist. On the one hand, a varying manner going from careful engraving to the most vivid etching, but always ample, always concerned with large luminous effects and reflecting a noble and monumental style. On the other hand, a great number of monotonous etchings in a finished manner but meagre and with a small-scale style. The only date we find in the second group, 1556 on plate 33 of the *Navigations*, leads us to believe that these prints are a little later than the others.

Are these two groups of such very different prints by the same printmaker, or is the presence of the same monogram a coincidence? We have long been uncertain but inclined towards the second solution. Indeed it is difficult to accept that the author of the magnificent prints after Primaticcio, one of the boldest etchers of the century, could have been reduced to such a timid style as that of the loves of Pluto series. There would appear to be confirmation for this in the attribution of the *Navigations orientales* illustrations to Louis Danet, whom Jean Adhémar distinguishes from Léon Davent.[2] This attribution originates from the *Bibliographie Lyonnaise* by Baudrier, who states that the figures in the *Navigations*

---

[1] Geneviève Monnier, *Le Seizième siècle européen – Dessins du Louvre*, exhibition catalogue (Paris 1966), pointed out the relationship of motif between the children's games seen in certain landscapes and in the group of drawings attributed by Otto Benesch to Jean Cousin the younger. This observation finds striking confirmation in a discovery kindly communicated to me by Philippe de Montebello, who will be publishing it shortly: the original design in reverse for the print Herbet No. 218, *Enfants jouant près d'une fontaine*, is in the British Museum under the name Jean Cousin. M. de Montebello, who has been doing a study of this artist, considered the attribution well-founded. We would add that this print, like Nos. 185, 201, 213-18, none of which bear the mark L.D., are very different in technique from the rest of the series, and are therefore, we believe, by another artist. It is not impossible that these prints, which have more refined draughtsmanship and a more colourful texture, with curly lines in the manner of the British Museum drawing, were executed by the author of the drawing himself.

[2] Jean Adhémar, *Inventaire du fonds français – Graveurs du XVIe siècle*, v. 2, Paris 1939, p. 281.

were etched by Louis Danet.[1] But he cites no supporting document and gives no earlier reference; he makes the statement as an accepted fact needing no explanation. Louis Danet, however, can be found nowhere before Baudrier. Natalis Rondot, who painstakingly combed the archives of Lyons and gave long lists of artists, did not find him, nor did Laborde in Paris, nor any other writer. All references to Louis Danet come solely from Baudrier. There are two possibilities: either Baudrier knew a document which he neglected to cite, or Louis Danet was born through an accident, the compositor or copyist having read Louis Danet for Léon Davent. The latter seems to us more probable.

If we must relegate Louis Danet to the limbo of fictitious artists, the problem of the two groups of prints remains as before and can only be resolved by an attentive study of the works. After having been in doubt for a long time, we are now convinced that the two groups are by the same artist, having found an intermediary in the series of *Capital Sins* (Pls LD 85–92), which will be discussed later. Nevertheless, except for a few examples, we have excluded the second group from this book. This may have been an arbitrary decision, but by eliminating some 125 pieces often of minor interest, it became possible to introduce others which provide a comparison shedding light directly on the problem of the Fontaine-bleau studio as we have proposed above to imagine it. The second part of the work by the supposed Daven, even if it is indeed by him, does not belong to the same category, because it dates from a later period and probably was not executed at Fontainebleau.

There are very few unmarked sheets which can clearly be attributed to L.D. We can deduce from this that the artist was in the habit of marking his works, and that attribution of the unsigned pieces must be undertaken with the utmost circumspection. Certain pieces that Herbet attributes to L.D. are assigned in this book to more plausible authors. *Abraham sacrifiant Isaac* will be found among the works of the supposed Jean Mignon (Pl. JM 54); this is true also of *Bataille sous Troie* (Pl. JM 42). *L'Eternel assis sur le globe* is surely by Fantuzzi (Pl. AF 64). We remain undecided about the attribution of *Nymphe regardant un héron s'envoler* (Pl. LD 37), which has much in common with some of L.D.'s works, such as *Jason tuant le dragon* (Pl. LD 16); but at the same time the method of modelling is different enough from all we know of him to leave doubts.

The chronology of L.D.'s works is difficult to establish because we lack guiding marks: the *Jeune femme habillée à l'antique* (Pl. LD3), an engraving of 1540; *Les Apôtres contemplant le Christ et la Vierge* of 1546; a certain number of pieces dated 1547; and finally a plate of *Navigations orientales* (Pl. LD 98) of 1556. This leaves a good deal of room for conjecture when it comes to placing the rest of his works, whose style often deviates from that of the dated pieces. But points of contact with other printmakers, particularly with Fantuzzi, permit certain hypotheses. We propose to reconstruct L.D.'s development in the following way: let us accept that the burin engravings can be placed at the beginning of his graphic activity. The *Jeune femme qui pleure (Psyché)* (Pl. LD 1) is so gross and clumsy in execution that it may be the earliest of his works that we know. It should be dated 1540 at the latest – a date which appears on the *Jeune femme habillée à l'antique*. On the other hand, we would place at the end of this period the *Hercule couché auprès d'Omphale* (Pl. LD 9), whose emphatic luminosity and complex hatching give evidence of new interests. This execution and the effect of the whole are very close to the work in the pendant to this composition, *Hercule se laissant habiller en femme* (Pl. LD 10), which is an etching. It seems probable that these two pieces are separated by a short interval, at a time when L.D. abandoned

---

[1] Henri Louis and Julien Baudrier, *Bibliographie Lyonnaise*, v. IX, p. 318.

engraving and devoted himself to etching. Other etchings are executed in the same style: the details are dense and complex, the bite of the acid is not deep and often shows accidents; the plate is imperfectly polished or perhaps even deliberately roughened, with cleaned parts to express light; certain effects are often obtained in the printing by wiping the plate insufficiently or irregularly. The most beautiful proofs of the series of goddesses and muses (Pls LD 25-36), which must be placed at the end of this period, are printed with a film of ink; this gives a tone to the whole sheet and helps to support the line, which is treated here with great economy. Two of L.D.'s etchings in this manner, the *Nymphe mutilant un satyre* (Pl. LD 15) and *Jason tuant le dragon* (Pl. LD 16), have pendants by Fantuzzi, *Jupiter et Antiope* (Pl. AF 71) and *Jason labourant le champ* (Pl. AF 69), in a very similar style – so much so that one might attribute them to the same etcher if they were not signed. We believe it must be accepted that these prints were executed by the two masters at the same period. If Fantuzzi's pieces were indeed done in 1544, that enables us to place L.D.'s etchings in the same year. L.D. would thus have begun etching in 1543 or 1544.

The next guidemark is the large print in four plates dated 1546. A great number of prints must be ascribed to the period between the first etchings and this one, but it is difficult to establish an exact order. One can grant that L.D.'s style evolved rapidly, parallel with that of Fantuzzi. The stroke is broader, the hatching less dense, the graphic system becomes more artificial, the plates are better polished, more deeply etched, and generally better wiped. A certain softness is introduced little by little into the style, such as one observes in the piece of 1546. We would readily place pieces such as the *Apollon du Belvédère* (Pl. LD 17) and the two antique statues in 1544-45; then about 1545 the beautiful oval etchings after compositions in the Chambre d'Alexandre. Then, perhaps in 1546, the rectangular *Jupiter et Sémélé* (Pl. LD 68); if one compares this print with the same subject in oval (Pl. LD 11), which goes with the earliest group of etchings, one can see all that separates the two styles. Both etchings are after Primaticcio, both are admirable, with impeccable drawing and perfect intelligence. The light is treated in both with particular care, but in one case it is diffuse, filtered, subtly modulated; the scene, whose elements fuse with one another, exists in a space that is vague, poetic and evocative. In the second version everything is more deliberate. The light is set by sharp contrasts of deep shadows and brilliant whites. The space is now very architectonic, the forms are drawn in it with precision. What L.D. has lost in delicacy and lightness, he has gained in power and plastic beauty, as in the superbly voluptuous body of Semele; what he has lost in poetry he has gained in decorative qualities.

Six sheets bear the date 1547. *Jupiter entouré des autres divinités* (Pl. LD 76) is the one which is closest to the work of 1546. This leads us to think that the differences which can be seen in other pieces of the same year, particularly the three oval prints representing hunting and fishing scenes (Pls LD 77-79) or the *Femme portée vers un satyre libidineux* (Pl. LD 81), indicate a new direction in L.D.'s art. Their style is simplified, more precise, the contour is more distinct. We must add to these certain other pieces, especially the *Christ aux Limbes* (Pl. LD. 84, which is entirely in this manner.

The important series of Capital Sins must be placed in this period or shortly after. The author of the designs is known by the inscription borne by the piece which serves as a sort of frontispiece to the series and which represents Justice with the seven sins chained to her belt. It is Luca Penni. And the recently discovered inventory made after his death shows that Luca Penni possessed the copperplates of this series.[1] The prints exist in two very different states which have not hitherto been distinguished. Judging

[1] Paul Vanaise, *op. cit.*

by the second state, we have long doubted the attribution of these pieces to L.D., though no one had questioned it up to then. The considerable part played by the burin, the almost Mantuan character of the works, the absence of any monogram on a series of such importance, seemed to us difficult to reconcile with an attribution to L.D. On the other hand, the first state, of which M. Paul Prouté owns a complete set, reverses the situation. With the exception of two plates, *La Luxure* and *La Paresse*, the prints of this state are entirely different – much lighter, exclusively etched or nearly so, and in a style which is much closer to that of the *Christ aux Limbes*. To remove all doubt about the attribution, the introductory piece bears the monogram quite legibly at bottom left.

La Luxure and *La Paresse*, however, were not altered from one edition to another. A comparison of these two pieces with the others in both of their different states leads to the following observations: one finds in *La Luxure*, as in all the other pieces in the second state, the work of L.D. – characterized by the treatment of the ground with little elements of vegetation – covered over everywhere by work with the burin in a Mantuan taste quite different from L.D.'s, but most skilful and without any of the grossness of ordinary restorers. The dark tone of this plate appears again in *La Paresse*, but one does not find in the latter L.D.'s typical dotted etching. The etching is mixed with engraving, but in a different balance. The general effect is harsher, the drawing rougher; a different sensitivity emerges. But the method of treating the ground, of crowding the shadows, appears again in *La Luxure* and in the other sheets of the second state. Certain conclusions can be drawn from this. The series of Capital Sins, essentially executed by L.D., was finished by another printmaker who retouched *La Luxure*, perhaps because the plate was incomplete, and who executed *La Paresse* himself. A probably small edition was published in this state. Then, perhaps because L.D.'s plates were too pale, or to give more unity to the series, the second artist retouched all the other plates. We cannot identify this anonymous artist.

The Capital Sins are represented in isolated ovals, each with four small circles in which Penni illustrated several examples or effects of the sin in question. It appears to us that the small circles etched by L.D. form a landmark between the two groups of his works. There can be no doubt at all that these plates were executed by Master L.D., whom we call Léon Daven. But the auxiliary subjects, particularly those in *L'Envie* which contain elements of landscape, offer striking resemblances to the series of the second group. We have already said that the Capital Sins series must be placed at the end of L.D.'s Fontainebleau career; perhaps indeed they were executed elsewhere. The two series etched after Léonard Thiry (the story of Callisto and the Pluto and Proserpine group), which come closest to the little subjects of the Capital Sins, could have been executed immediately afterwards. Despite the charm of Thiry's compositions, there is something routine in these plates; they lack the inspiration which animated the works of the preceding period, and one would not know how to explain this transformation except for a change of environment.

This entirely mysterious man was certainly not a great genius. If he was able (for a time, at least) to be Marcantonio to Primaticcio, he was not able to sustain such a high level. One feels that he not only required a great model, but also the enthusiasm of the moment, in order to attain poetry. Without that – in his Oriental costumes, in his small animated landscapes – he sank into the ordinary. But his best pieces – *Jason tuant le dragon*, the two versions of *Sémélé*, the oval hunting and fishing scenes of 1547 – have a boldness of touch, a luminous effect, a lightness without peer among his contemporaries and rarely equalled.

Jean Mignon is today considered one of the principal Fontainebleau printmakers. A number of pieces are attributed to him, all of them very well drawn, with a rather cold elegance, a cerebral sensibility – if one might use such an expression. The fact that his name is indisputably French has caused him to be regarded as one of the earliest representatives of French classicism. This fine master, however, poses extremely delicate problems, and these must be raised in order to explain the choice of works here, which diverges from earlier presentations. The reader will perhaps excuse a report which may be tedious but is indispensable to the question.

We know of two pieces signed by Jean Mignon. One (Pl. JM 7), bearing the date 1544, is a free rendering of a stucco decoration by Primaticcio which still exists in the chamber of Mme d'Etampes at Fontainebleau. The other (Pl. JM 8) is an historical subject which remains obscure. According to Bartsch, followed by Herbet, it represents 'a woman bearing gifts to a prince'. It is, in fact, an old man who holds a scale in which he is having weighed the contents of a bag in front of a man seated under a canopy. Since the latter is a captain surrounded by soldiers, the subject must be the payment of a ransom rather than an offering of gifts. These two pieces are very accurately drawn, the execution colourful and lively in a very refined taste. Their author, Jean Mignon, is also known to us through a reference in the Fontainebleau accounts of 1537-40. He worked as a painter and was paid 13 *livres* a month; since the principal assistants received 20 *livres* this would make him an artist of the second rank. There is no reason to question the identification of our etcher with the painter employed at the Château. The artist later established himself in Paris, where in 1552 he had unsuccessfully stood for election to the jury of master-painters.

This is all that one knows positively about Jean Mignon. But Mariette, who knew the piece dated 1544, already stated, 'This is the only piece I have ever seen with this artist's name; it may well be that a number of pieces etched in France at about this time and bearing no name are by this artist. It is worth investigating.' Bartsch took up the suggestion. He did not find the piece described by Mariette, for he speaks only of the other signed plate; on the other hand, he knew Mariette's note, which led to the suggestion of Mignon as the author of a certain number of anonymous prints. But Bartsch's effort was hindered by the fact that he attributed to a mythical printmaker, Florent Despesches, a number of works now attributed to Mignon. Renouvier corrected Bartsch's error. He mentions a number of pieces which he attributes to Mignon without attempting to draw up a complete list, and he was the first to characterize the master's work. 'Mignon nibbles as he etches, but has infinitely less effect and vividness [than L.D.]; and he remains incomparable in the ferocity of his expressions and the strangeness of his gestures; the severe working of his hatching and stipple resembles nothing so much as the embroiderer's art. Moreover, he has the ungainly forms and choreographic attitudes of the School, and his peculiar traits are the gimlet eyes in gaping holes and the jutting jaws.'[1] Renouvier had also grouped under the name 'Etcher of Luca Penni' a certain number of prints which are at present attributed to Mignon. It is not without interest to cite his analysis. 'He is grandiose in his drawing, and the severe expression and subtle workmanship are his alone; his figures are still wild, but grave; the flesh is modelled, the drapery supple, and the care and richness he gives to the trees and plants can be seen in no other etcher

[1] Jules Renouvier, *Des types et des manières . . . XVIe siècle,* Montpellier 1854, pp. 184-85 and 187.

26

of the School. He is less of a draughtsman than Fantuzzi, less pleasant than Thiry [i.e. L.D.], less wild than Vignay [Master I. ♀.V.] and Mignon. His typical figures, which might easily be taken for Luca Penni's, provide a pattern of the beauty of Fontainebleau, more solid than Primaticcio's figures, more guarded than Rosso's.'

Herbet deserves the credit for having drawn together the two groups of works which form the basis for his catalogue of Jean Mignon. This catalogue was the starting-point for Jules Lieure who devoted a great deal of attention to the study of Jean Mignon, an artist for whom he felt a special affection. Unfortunately he was unable to complete his work. Nevertheless several indications published in a general work and notes deposited in the Cabinet des Estampes permit us to form an idea of what Lieure planned.[1] He intended a catalogue of 75 items, whereas Herbet described only 27. Lieure placed Mignon's career as a printmaker between 1543 and 1545. For the rest, his analysis had not yet got very far, and he left very few precise indications on the subject of chronology.

We have made use of Lieure's valuable notes, even though diverging on many points. But before discussing the reconstitution which we suggest, it is necessary to stress its uncertainties. It is not an easy task to establish relationships between a body of prints extending over several years and two rather unimportant signed pieces, whose author is otherwise almost unknown. The chances of error are increased when dealing with an extremely fertile environment in which one finds several printmakers working in closely related styles. The very fact that Jean Mignon's signature appears so completely on two pieces which are relatively unimportant in comparison with many of those attributed to him must arouse suspicion – all the more as these two signed pieces are more finely drawn and in a more colourful manner than any other in the group.

Nonetheless, the reasons for preserving a good many of the attributions made to Mignon seem to us adequate. If, for example, one compares the grass and architectural elements in the background of the signed piece with similar elements in the backgrounds of prints on the Trojan War, such as *Le perfide Sinon* (Pl. JM 43) or *Le Pillage de Troie* (Pl. JM 45), the correspondence is striking and significant, because those are characteristic traits of the printmaker. There is enough kinship in the general taste of the drawing, in the method of softening the features of the faces with their grim look and the gimlet-like eyes of the full-face figures, to confirm us in our conviction.

Mignon's work consists above all of a very solid nucleus of prints grouped around a series of six sheets on the history of Troy (Pls JM 40–45). The homogeneity of this ensemble, however, is independent of its relation to the pieces signed by Mignon. Their manner is ample, full of air, assured, and not without resemblances to that of Master L.D. – indeed, so much so that in Herbet's book the *Bataille sous Troie* is found in the catalogue of L.D. although it is indisputably part of Mignon's series. Fortunately the Louvre has several of Penni's original drawings for this series. The drawings are the reverse of the prints. The very exact correspondence between the drawing and the print, at least so far as the figures are concerned, makes one believe that these are the very drawings used by the etcher, who followed them with scrupulous fidelity. Hence it is revealing to notice in what ways Mignon diverges from his model or completes it. This takes place invariably in the landscape and natural features. In the background of *Le perfide Sinon introduit par les bergers,* he has placed a landscape of his own invention with trees bearing

---

[1] Jules Lieure, *op. cit.,* pp. 83–86, which must be supplemented by the manuscript notes in the Cabinet des Estampes. As far as can be judged, the notes must be in about the same state they were in when Lieure wrote his manual.

very peculiar leaves and ruins covered with vegetation. Even in *Les Troyens introduisant le cheval de bois*, in which there was hardly room for interpretation, he creates crevices in the walls and has his characteristic vegetation growing out of them.

One can see the same motif in another piece undoubtedly etched by the same master, the *Portement de croix* (Pl. JM 29); the original design by Penni is also in the Louvre. The etcher has meticulously follow the indications of the drawing. But in the foreground, a space left almost empty by the designer is filled with a bounding dog and with elements of vegetation. It is these elements and the master's original way of treating landscape – his sentiment of nature, so to speak – that justify most of our attributions.

In addition to the aforementioned prints, there are a number of sheets in which Jean Mignon's hand can be recognized beyond doubt: *La Création d'Eve* (Pl. JM 56), *La Tentation d'Eve* (Pl. JM 57), *Saint Jean prêchant au désert* (Pl. JM 55), two *Adoration des mages* (Pls JM 39, 49), the *Last Judgment* (Pl. JM 52), *Cléopâtre piquée par un aspic* (Pl. JM 31), *Marcus Curtius se précipitant dans un gouffre* (Pl. JM 48), the *Mort d' Adonis* (Pl. JM 53), the *Enlèvement de Proserpine* (Pl. JM 32), *Femmes au bain* (Pl. JM 46), *Vénus au bain servie par les nymphes* (Pl. JM 34), the *Métamorphose d'Actéon* (Pl. JM 60), *Entellus et Darès* (Pl. JM 51), *Combat d'hommes nus* (Pl. JM 33). Other pieces are sufficiently close in style to be attributed without too much hesitation: for example, *Saint Michel combattant les anges rebelles* (Pl. JM 50) and several pieces of ornamentation. We believe, as Lieure did, that we must add to these a beautiful set of twenty Terminals (statues of the type used for the god Terminus). These are catalogued by Herbet as anonymous burin engravings, but one cannot understand why, since etching clearly predominates.

In our view one must also attribute to Jean Mignon a very rare print of Andrea del Sarto's *La Charité* (Pl. JM 6). The natural elements, which are entirely different from those in the painting, seem to us in Mignon's taste, and a comparison of the detail with the *Portement de croix* definitely confirms the attribution. The two pieces bear the same date, 1544. The attribution of *La Charité* necessarily entails that of the *Sainte Famille aux oiseaux* (Pl. JM 5), thanks to the same comparisons. In this context one will also notice the resemblance between the landscapes in this plate and the one in the background of *Jugement de Pâris*; in spite of the etching technique, the design of the buildings and the treatment of the road leading to them reveal the same taste and feeling.

Lieure believed Mignon's beginnings as a printmaker were to be found in a group of sheets, one of which, *La Mort d'Hylas* (Herbet, No. 54 anonymous), is dated 1543. Despite certain coincidences in the natural elements, particularly the tufts of grass, we believe that one must reject from this master's œuvre prints of clumsy and unrefined draughtsmanship, whose feeling is unlike Mignon's, especially in the relationship between figures and background.

The Mignon of 1543 must be sought elsewhere, and we believe he is to be found in a beautiful print, dated that year, representing *La Sainte Famille* (Pl. JM 1). The taste of the design, the method of strongly linking the figures to the background, of treating the draperies in a geometric and decorative way, have much in common with the rest of the œuvre. The mask in the upper centre has the 'gimlet eyes'. In its quality and feeling, this piece is also in harmony with *La Sainte Famille* (Pl. JM 4) which Renouvier already attributed to Mignon and which must be dated at about the same time. Perhaps *La Sainte Famille* with the ornamented crib (Pl. JM 3) should also be added to them. One need not be too surprised by all these variations on the same theme, of which we shall find an entirely contemporary example in the *Nativités* by Dumoûtier. What is more difficult is to determine the author of the designs. By the grandeur of its conception, the composition dated 1543 makes one think of Primaticcio. But the figures and the sense of space, as well as the print's kinship with those that follow and are not after Primaticcio, lead us to seek another master. One print very close to this group, probably executed by Mignon but not reproduced here because the print itself is lost and known only through a poor reproduction of the nineteenth century, bears the inscription 'I.C. inven.'[1] Are we to see in this the name of Jean Cousin, as Mariette and Firmin-Didot did? A comparison of a print signed by Cousin, the *Mise au Tombeau*, leads us to believe this is true. And should we, then, attribute to this artist the conception of these most interesting prints by Jean Mignon? That would be not only a considerable contribution to the highly problematic work of Cousin, but also an extremely interesting link between the master of Sens and the School of Fontainebleau.

In the absence of guidemarks, the chronology of Jean Mignon's work is hard to reconstruct. Lieure thought it possible to confine his graphic work to the years 1543 to 1545. Surely he was not far out: 1543 is probably the date for the earliest etchings, i.e. the variations on the Holy Family, and perhaps also *Vénus au bain* (Pl. JM 34), which is difficult to place. Four pieces bear the date 1544: the signed and dated print of ornamentation; *La Charité*, which resembles it in style (note particularly the modelling of the children); the *Portement de croix* and the *Enlèvement de Proserpine*. We believe the *Sainte Famille aux oiseaux* is slightly earlier than *La Charité*. The *Bataille d'hommes nus* seems to be contemporary with the *Portement de croix*, and perhaps also with the *Cléopâtre* and the *Rançon du corps d'Hector*. The rest of the work was undoubtedly done later. *Entellus et Darès*, *Marcus Curtius* and the framed *Adoration des Mages* (Pl. JM 49) seem to fit quite naturally after the Trojan War series. That series marks the moment when Mignon approached closest to L.D., and in this period must be placed the unframed *Adoration des Mages* (Pl. JM 39), which is one of the master's greatest successes. We would also put here the *Présentation de la Vierge* after Giulio Romano, a work one might attribute to L.D. were it not for the way the whole composition is brought to the surface and for a slightly different manner of placing the shadows and treating the white of the banister. Later the master's style was to become more complicated. His workmanship became increasingly complex and systematic. If this development of his style is accepted, we must place between the *Guerre de Troie* and *Actéon*, which we believe shows the master's final style, such pieces as the *Last Judgment* or the *Femmes au bain*. The fine and delicate workmanship of these pieces is confirmed in *Abraham sacrifiant Isaac* and *La Mort d'Adonis*, in which Eros is treated in stipple. This experiment is pushed much farther in *La Prédication de saint Jean* which seems to us, along with *Actéon* and *La Tentation d'Eve*, one of the last pieces executed by the master. It is very difficult to assign a date to these works. But judging by the general development of etching at Fontainebleau, it is unlikely that this date is much later than 1547; we doubt that it is prior to 1546 for the same reasons, and also in order to leave sufficient time for the transformation in the artist's style.

Jean Mignon remains, above all, the etcher of Luca Penni. Most of the prints he left us were designed by this artist, for whom he showed a perfect sympathy. But for the constant transformation of the landscapes between the drawings and the etchings, one might even wonder if these etchings were not Penni's own work, since according to Vasari he made prints. There must have been a regular collaboration between the two artists, and one would like to have more information on the circumstances of this

---

[1] Ambroise Firmin-Didot, *Recueil des œuvres choisies de Jean Cousin*, Paris 1873.

production, which remain entirely obscure. Some have sought to credit Jean Mignon with the invention of the rich frames around many of his prints; but this is not possible. The drawing of *La Mort d'Adonis* in the Teyler Museum at Haarlem bears the frame, and the fact that the landscape differs from that in the print shows that this is a case of an original drawing and not a preparation by Mignon. Another drawing by Penni in the Louvre (Inv. 1396), of which no print is known, also shows the remains of such a frame, which has unfortunately been cut. We must therefore believe that the frames were Penni's work. On the other hand, we think that Mignon was the inventor, or at least the compiler and adapter, of the series of Terminals, which draws on various sources. One is an exact repeat of the right-hand part of *Marcus Curtius* and was therefore probably derived from Penni. Two come from the *Termes* of Agostino Veneziano, two others from Bonasone. Most of the others probably had similar origins. But Mignon breathes into all this a Gallic spirit, a vivacious and almost mischievous humour which makes something extremely amusing of this series.

Jean Mignon is inferior to Master L.D. only in the inequality of his models. As an etcher, he has no cause to envy L.D. Two characteristics are constant in him: the authority, indeed the power of his drawing; and the graphic unity of his plates. The latter consists, above all, of an almost equal distribution of accents all over the plate and of a method of linking the figures to their background through the quality of the line. At first lively, vivid and even violent, Mignon's style changed with time, became disciplined and led to grandiose effects which improved upon the cold beauty of Luca Penni. In the large prints of his late period, Mignon made use of varied, complex and expert techniques, unusual light, and arrested gestures. He installed his figures in very contrived, very formal landscapes with artificial vegetation. The result was an unreal world, as if turned to stone, one of the most uncompromising expressions of mannerism.

ORIGINAL PRINTMAKERS:

GEOFFROY DUMOÛTIER, LÉONARD LIMOSIN, THE SUPPOSED JUSTE DE JUSTE

With Jean Mignon we leave those printmakers who interpreted the work of painters and take up certain artists who made prints from their own compositions. Thus we touch on an aspect of the School of Fontainebleau which is little known and difficult to recover: the personal work of minor artists who gravitated around the major Italian decorators. Mariette had already noted that it was a matter of interest to see in Dumoûtier's etchings the course that a French artist could derive from the example of Rosso.[1] The same is true of the extremely rare etchings of Léonard Limosin. Finally the strange etchings by the monogrammist sometimes called Juste and sometimes Viset show us the extreme of eccentricity permitted in this artistic environment. The inventions of these artists remain incontestably inferior to those of Rosso or Primaticcio, or even Luca Penni. Nevertheless, they are personal, sometimes excessively so, and have a liveliness and independence of spirit which make them not only engaging but also most valuable in forming a true idea of the peripheral art of Fontainebleau.

Geoffroy Dumoûtier is the earliest representative of a family of artists which produced several well-known portraitists, the last of whom, Daniel, worked in the mid-seventeenth century. Geoffroy

---

[1] Jean-Pierre Mariette, *Abecedario*, v. 2, Paris 1853-54, pp. 129-30.

Dumoûtier came from Rouen, where he is mentioned as a miniaturist. The Fontainebleau accounts also refer to him between 1537 and 1540 as an assistant to Rosso.[1] This assures us of his participation in the work at Fontainebleau, but his salary of 13 *livres* a month puts him in the second category of assistants. He died in Paris in 1573. His would be nothing but a name among so many others if something of his work had not, by good fortune, been preserved. A group of etchings bear his name.[2] It is not etched into the plate, but written with a pen, and always by the same hand. Since the spelling 'Dumonstier' is the same as that used by the members of the family themselves, and different from the phonetic spelling Dumoûtier found elsewhere, and since, moreover, one finds more than one proof of the same plate inscribed this way, there are good reasons to believe that this is a signature rather than inscriptions added by a collector.

The prints by Dumoûtier are in a highly personal style making it possible for us to attribute to him several sheets of which no signed proofs have been preserved. At present we know of twenty etchings by Geoffroy Dumoûtier; the Bibliothèque Nationale has a complete collection of these. In some cases we know of only a single impression. They are all of religious or allegorical subjects.

Dumoûtier is constantly inspired by Rosso – in his characters, his costumes, his manner of composing in the picture plane and not in space, and even in violence of effect, which he exaggerates. The biting of his plates is particularly careless, to the point that certain pieces can barely be made out – although it does not seem that these are later impressions. As a printmaker Dumoûtier was influenced by Fantuzzi above all. He even outdoes the abruptness and the unnatural light effects that Fantuzzi affected in 1542. The date 1543, which appears on *La Vierge* (Pl. GD 12), proves that Dumoûtier followed his model by only a short interval. At the end of his career as an etcher, Dumoûtier diverged from the violent style of his beginnings in four pieces etched with more care, in which stipple is mixed with line to soften the overall effect. The figures are more plastic, and Primaticcio's influence can now be felt, particularly in *La Justice* (Pl. GD 25). In sum, between 1543 and 1547, the date on *Allégorie* (Pl. GD 23), Dumoûtier followed a development similar to that of Fantuzzi or Mignon. The pieces in his early manner, however, are far more numerous than the others, and one does not sense a continuous development. It may be that he produced the bulk of his etchings in two distinct periods, one around 1543, the other in 1547, with perhaps a few sheets, such as *L'Eglise* (?) (Pl. GD 22), which seem to be somewhere in between.

Dumoûtier is a bold designer, exceptionally decisive and almost profound. It is true that his repertory of forms is limited, that his angular flat faces are repeated from one print to another. But he knew how to compose. In his series of Nativities, surely etched at only short intervals of one another, he succeeded in skilfully varying the grouping of figures, and obtained powerful effects through unusual light. What was Dumoûtier capable of as a painter? We cannot say, since there are no examples, but his most successful etchings show that he had the makings of a true artist, capable – at least in a restricted format – of giving a personal interpretation of Italian models. Several drawings and a miniature attributed to him fully confirm this impression.

[1] Laborde, *op. cit.*, v. 1, p. 137.

[2] These prints were catalogued by Robert-Dumesnil, *Le Peintre-Graveur français*, v. 5, Paris 1841, pp. 33-44, with supplement by Georges Duplessis, v. 11, p. 84; a supplementary piece in André Linzeler, *Inventaire du fonds français – Graveurs du XVIe siècle*, v. 1, Paris 1932.

The name of Léonard Limosin is almost synonymous with enamel painting, that iridescent art which thrived in Limoges during the sixteenth century and of which countless examples still exist everywhere. He is believed to have been born in Limoges around 1505, and he died in the same city between 1575 and 1577. He had a brother, Martin Limosin, also an enamel painter, with whom he seems to have collaborated. Léonard practised enamel painting in all its forms: plaques with religious or mythological subjects, retables, dishes, etc. His speciality was portraits, and he represented all the famous figures of his day, adapting crayon drawings by the Clouets and their circle. The enamels are generally a good deal inferior to the sketches in the quality of their design and their lack of naturalness. But if one considers the difficulty of the technique, one is surprised by Léonard's virtuosity, and these portraits with porcelain skin were immensely popular, which proves their charm. In the course of his long career as enameller to the King, Léonard Limosin received the most important commissions of the period and gained a universal reputation which eclipsed that of rivals who may have been just as talented as he.

Léonard did not devote himself entirely to enamel. He was also a painter, and was summoned to Bordeaux in that capacity to prepare decorations for a royal entry in 1564. The museum at Limoges has a large picture by him, *L'Incrédulité de saint Thomas*, signed and dated 1551; it is a rather mediocre work, but valuable, because of its rarity, as an example of French painting in that period.

Finally, we know of eight etchings by Léonard Limosin, and it may be that he did others, for the impressions that are known are, for the most part, unique.[1] These pieces are in a completely unified style, and since the date 1544 appears on several of them we may surmise that the whole series was done in that year. Each piece is signed, either with the full name or with the customary monogram of the enameller, L.L. Technical and stylistic links enable us to presume and almost affirm that these etchings were executed at the time of a visit to Fontainebleau.

There is no comprehensive study of the work of this great enameller who, as artisans usually do, drew his ideas from various sources, thanks particularly to prints. At the beginning he was attracted by Northern as much as Italian art, and in 1532 he borrowed several scenes from Dürer's *Small Passion*. But with time he was to devote himself entirely to Italian art and especially that of Fontainebleau. His connections with the court no doubt had something to do with this, and it is probable that he was accepted as a pioneer among the enamellers of Limoges. It is known that in 1545 he received the commission for the twelve apostles now at Saint-Père in Chartres, executed from the cartoons of Michel Rochetel, who himself used preliminary sketches by Primaticcio. This commission mentions arrangements made verbally, which vouches for Limosin's presence at court. Maybe the etchings of 1544 were done during the same visit.

These prints, all of which represent episodes in the life of Christ and probably constitute a series, are interesting to compare with those of Dumoûtier. Léonard, with infinitely less talent, gives a similar interpretation of the same models. There is the same Rosso manner in his work, the same angularity of the heads, the same excessive and violent character. For example, one can observe the way he suppresses the chin on the faces of old men with agitated beards. But Léonard is a poor draughtsman. The extremities of the figures are often gross, the faces deformed, the draperies lacking in skill. Nor does he have that understanding of effect which allows Dumoûtier to make the best of his faulty technique.

---

[1] André Demartial, 'Léonard Limosin, émailleur et graveur', *Revue de l'Art Chrétien*, LXII, 1912, pp. 18–28, describes Limosin's known prints and gives a report on the related enamels, of which some are reproduced.

Limosin's compositions give the impression of a jigsaw of figures borrowed from here and there. The two figures on the right of the *Résurrection* (Pl. LL 8), for example, are borrowed literally from a composition by Rosso, or more probably an etching of 1543 derived from it.[1]

Léonard Limosin's attempt to furnish his own inventions – sometimes with a certain success, as in *Jesus-Christ renvoyé par Hérode* (Pl. LL 7) – is interesting in itself. He must have cut the figure of a great man in his region, a sort of Jean Cousin of the south-west. In our eyes, brilliant as he may have been at enamelling, Limosin remains a mediocre artist, but very curious because of his provincialism furbished with Fontainebleau novelties. The fact that he repeated exactly several of his 1544 prints in enamels of 1557 (now in the Musée de Cluny) may show that in the long run routine prevailed over curiosity.

Now we come to a group of works, as mysterious as strange, which closes our selection of etchers. We reproduce here seventeen prints representing academic figures in a completely extravagant manner. A series of twelve plates shows these figures in isolation, the other series of five groups them in astonishing gymnastic pyramids. These violent etchings, which consensus places in the School of Fontainebleau, have surprised everyone by the strangeness of their contorted figures, their violence of expression, their originality and their isolation.

The five prints of human pyramids bear a monogram formed of several letters. Renouvier was the first to suggest a possible interpretation by reading the word IUSTE or Juste, all the letters of which appear in the monogram. This would involve Juste de Juste, assistant to Rosso at Fontainebleau and member of a famous family of sculptors. But a document discovered by B. Fillon led Arnauldet to suggest another candidate.[2] The text in question concerns the division of an inheritance of a wealthy goldsmith in Fontenay-le-Comte; it contains the names of two artists. One is 'Noël Garnier painctre, demourant à Paris'. We know of a group of engravings signed Noël Garnier; since the period corresponds, there is no room for doubt that this is the same artist. The other one is 'Jehan Viset, graveur et tailleur d'hystoires en cuivre de present à Fontainebleau, on service de Mgr de la Vauguyon'. It was quite natural for Arnauldet to perceive in this the author of the gymnastic figures, for the name Viset, as well as Juste, is formed from the letters of the monogram. Herbet, who did not know Arnauldet's article, held that Renouvier's identification was probable, but Jean Adhémar and other writers who knew of Arnauldet have stuck to Viset.

Tempting as the identification may be, the picture we get of Jean Viset in the document hardly suits the character of the prints in question. It should be noted first of all that Noël Garnier, described as a painter ('painctre'), appears as the most 'artistic' of a family of artisans which included two goldsmiths, whereas Jean Viset, as a printmaker ('graveur'), seems to be more of a craftsman. Also, among the heirs it is Jean Viset to whom are left the 'outilz, oustillements et engins de mestier du dict defunct', which would indicate that he had a use for these craft tools. At the date of the document, 1536, as far as we can tell, etching was not practised at Fontainebleau; it appeared there first in 1542. Everything indicates that Jean Viset was an engraver, a printmaker by profession. Now the etchings sometimes attributed to

---

[1] *Un homme tenant un masque, accompagné de diverses figures et d'animaux*, Bartsch No. 85 anonymous; attributed to Fantuzzi by Herbet (No. 42); we give our reasons for rejecting this attribution in our introduction to the list of Fantuzzi's works.

[2] Thomas Arnauldet, 'Noël Garnier et Jean Viset, orfèvres-graveurs en taille-douce', *Archives de l'Art français*, 1861, pp. 357–69.

him are also as 'artistic' as possible, remarkable for their freedom and hasty technique. One has the impression of an artist who makes prints only *en passant*. Apart from the figures we reproduce here, there is nothing else that can be attributed to the same hand, which is, however, so personal that it would identify the rest of the work if any existed. Besides, a series of figures engraved after designs of the same master bears the monogram M.N., which indicates that they were executed by another printmaker.[1] We believe that all these factors make it virtually impossible to attribute the gymnastic figures to the engraver of Fontenay-le-Comte.

The document remains very interesting for it attests the presence of an engraver at Fontainebleau in 1536. But since we cannot identify his work, it is difficult to assess the importance of this fact. As for our etchings, once again they are left without an author. Perhaps we must revert to Renouvier's old attribution. Herbet writes justly: 'The ungainly attitudes, the exaggeration of the muscalature, above all the simplicity of the composition which eliminates every inessential detail, are appropriate to the idea that these prints were done by a sculptor rather than a painter, and makes the attribution proposed by M. Renouvier acceptable.' It is impossible to support this with anything more positive, for we know of no work by Juste de Juste.

Whoever the author of these plates may be, they are still one of the curious documents of the period as the limit that personal eccentricity could reach in an atmosphere which particularly lent itself to this. The human pyramids make one think quite naturally of certain compositions by Bertos. They are less elegant but also less affected and, in a way, their mannerism is less mannered. These few prints are not by a great artist, and some monotony already creeps into this restricted output; but they are by a clever draughtsman and a great original who was able to state the impossible with conviction.

THE ENGRAVERS: PIERRE MILAN, DOMENICO DEL BARBIERE

If the question of the Fontainebleau etchings may seem complex, that of the engravings is even more obscure. It is not always easy to see which of them were executed at Fontainebleau, at Paris, in Italy or in Flanders. Because of the almost total lack of dated pieces, it is impossible to establish a chronology, and the similarity of styles, at least among those which seem to have been executed at Paris, is such that the attribution of anonymous sheets is entirely uncertain. Engravings which reflect the art of Fontainebleau were executed in Paris without any perceptible change of style over a long period. Since Robert-Dumesnil's catalogue[2] almost all of this output has been ascribed to René Boyvin. However, a document discovered by Yves Metman put the subject in question again, for it proved that several important works attributed to Boyvin were in fact by a printmaker who until then was nothing but a name – Pierre Milan.[3]

[1] But not René Boyvin, as is generally said. The engravings in the collection of M. Paul Prouté and the Albertina, Vienna, bear this monogram. We cannot say what name they stand for, but in any case it is not Boyvin.

[2] A. P. F. Robert-Dumesnil, *Le Peintre-Graveur français*, v. 8, Paris 1850, pp. 11-88.

[3] Yves Metman, 'Un graveur inconnu de l'Ecole de Fontainebleau: Pierre Milan', *Humanisme et Renaissance*, I, 1941, pp. 202-14.

34

The document is an inventory made after the death of a certain Claude Bernard, retired registrar of Provins settled in Paris. This text deserves a fairly detailed analysis. It shows us Pierre Milan, engraver on copper, constantly accruing debts and pledging his prints with moneylenders. He is closely associated with Marc Béchot who, in certain cases, stands pledge for him; less impecunious, he appears in the guise of guarantor. We know besides that, when he became general engraver of coins, Béchot took Pierre Milan on as first clerk. But this did not help Milan to discharge his debts either. In 1545 he borrowed money from Claude Bernard and, in order to obtain this loan, he pledged five engraved plates. But Claude Bernard was not his only creditor. In 1547 François Clouet, the famous portraitist, had assigned the outstanding debts of Marc Béchot and Pierre Milan to Guillaume Morlaye, well known as a music publisher. Then in 1549 Pierre Milan borrowed another 80 *écus* directly from Guillaume Morlaye and pledged eleven plates in exchange. We shall see that the plates which were the object of these transactions appeared later in Claude Bernard's house. In 1550 Pierre Milan sold Claude Bernard 250 copies of a series of twenty *Amours des dieux*.[1] Finally, on 3 March 1553, there was an agreement between Guillaume Morlaye and René Boyvin for the completion of the two unfinished plates by Pierre Milan 'bien et duement comme il apartiendra suivant le commancement, du portraict qui a esté imprimé sur lesdites lames imparfaictes'. This probably means that Milan had engraved the whole composition in outline, as engravers usually do. Metman skilfully showed that the two plates had come to Guillaume Morlaye with the debts assigned by Clouet because they are not among the twelve pledged in 1549. René Boyvin immediately received half the payment, i.e. 34 *livres* 10 *sols*. Then a year later, on 15 February 1554, he received the other half, not from Morlaye this time, but from Claude Bernard, who must have bought the plates from Morlaye in the meantime. Upon his death in 1557, Claude Bernard left all the engravings ranged in a chest and René Boyvin was charged with assessing the property. This consisted not only of the plates but also of impressions which Claude Bernard evidently had made. It is clear that he had been selling them; thus Claude Bernard appears as publisher of all these plates by Pierre Milan. Also in 1557, Pierre Milan was associated with René Boyvin in appraising prints and engraved copperplates of the inventory taken after Luca Penni's death.

This glance at the relationship of a close network including several known people gives us an idea of the environment in which Paris artists lived in the sixteenth century. A society turned in on itself, in which the same people are constantly meeting, a world in which art and trade are intimately linked, it was also no doubt just as distinctive an environment but quite different from the hierarchical world that one senses at Fontainebleau.

This important document not only allows us to discover a picturesque figure and his entourage; the naming of the plates is precise enough to enable us to identify them without ambiguity – at least

[1] Y. Metman, *op. cit.*, suggests identifying these plates with a series of ornamental compositions which contain the gods of fable after Léonard Thiry. But the title *Amours des Dieux*, even with the restriction 'commonly so-called', does not fit Thiry's compositions. These *Amours des dieux* are probably copies of a series executed by Jacopo Caraglio after Rosso and Perino del Vago (Bartsch XV, No. 9–23; incomplete set). A complete series of copies in the free reserve of the Cabinet des Estampes under the name of Boyvin is perhaps really Pierre Milan's series; it bears Italian captions. There is another possible identification in a series in reverse (i.e. in the same direction as Caraglio's originals) of which an incomplete group (seven pieces) are in the Cabinet des Estampes among the works of Ducerceau. These rather brilliant engravings do not resemble anything else of Ducerceau's. Finally, a reduced copy with Italian captions, of which there is an incomplete group also in the free reserve, appears to be a copy made at Lyons after the prints kept under the name of Boyvin. The series obviously had a great success in France.

in certain cases. We can recognize the *Danse des dryades* (Pl. PM 1) after Rosso, *Jupiter et Calisto* (Pl. PM 4) after Primaticcio, and the plates finished by Boyvin: *Clélie* (Pl. PM 6) after Giulio Romano, and *La Nymphe de Fontainebleau* (Pl. PM 7) after Rosso. This is enough to give us an idea of Pierre Milan's style. It has power and brilliance. His cut is deep, direct, unconstrained and unhesitating. The graphic system is simple and strictly organized. The impression is regular; contrary to what one finds in the etchings, his plates are clean and carefully wiped, and his cuts, which are not very dense, come up cleanly on the white paper. The effect is of an extreme distinctness, and the decorative effect is accentuated through simple modelling and strong contours. There is something of the goldsmith and the artisan in this work, expressed in an insistence on the properly graphic qualities of the prints. Moreover, we are dealing with a professional handling so disciplined that it is perfectly transmitted. In the two pieces started by Pierre Milan and finished by Boyvin, it is impossible to say who did what, and certain plates signed by Boyvin are in a style entirely similar to those attested to be by Milan.

Jean Adhémar has suggested that Pierre Milan should be identified with the printmaker Pierre de la Cuffle.[1] In speaking of Augustin Jorisz, Van Mander declares: 'In the latter city [Paris] he settled in the home of M. Pierre de la Cuffle, excellent engraver on copper, who, among other prints, did *Les Trois Grâces* after Rosso, and a square ceiling seen in perspective. He was not a painter, but maintained a household with one of his brothers who employed in a permanent fashion, besides several goldsmiths, a painter and a sculptor; through them, Augustin found employment.'[2] According to Van Mander's information, Augustin would have stayed with Pierre de la Cuffle from 1547 to 1552, dates which correspond to Milan's period of activity. *Les Trois Grâces* after Rosso seems to be an error for *Les Parques nues*. On the other hand, among a number of unmarked engravings there is one plate, representing *Jupiter au milieu des Olympiens* (Pl. PM 5) after Primaticcio, the style of which is consistent with that of Pierre Milan. Ceilings viewed from below are sufficiently rare among prints to make it seem likely that this is in fact the plate referred to by Van Mander. These observations speak strongly in favour of the identification proposed by Adhémar. However, the position of Pierre de la Cuffle in his brother's prosperous establishment is hard to reconcile with Pierre Milan's constant money difficulties, which are proved by the documents. The identification of the plates mentioned by Van Mander is uncertain because of the vagueness of his descriptions. The long-sanctioned confusion between Milan and Boyvin must make us cautious, and even though the identification of Pierre Milan with Van Mander's Pierre de la Cuffle seems likely, it requires confirmation and must remain hypothetical.

Was engraving practised at Fontainebleau itself? It seems quite probable; at least one well-known artist of the Fontainebleau staff, Domenico del Barbiere, has left us a certain number of examples in this technique. This small œuvre of engravings makes him one of the masters of printmaking. Bartsch knew only nine pieces; Passavant added three, of which two are unfortunately known to us only by his description. To these Herbet added various prints, not all of which are convincing. One group of ornaments, the introductory piece of which is signed (Pl. DB 12), are certainly by Domenico. But Herbet confused Domenico's plates with copies in reverse and etched, which Renouvier attributes, probably correctly, to Ducerceau. Unfortunately we know only seven original prints by Domenico, but we may presume that the rest of the copies correspond to lost originals; that is why we reproduce them here.

---

[1] Jean Adhémar, 'Pierre Milan et les origines de l'Ecole de Fontainebleau', *Gazette des Beaux Arts*, May 1953, pp. 361 ff.
[2] Henri Hymans, *Le Livre des peintres de Carel Van Mander*, Paris 1884, v. I, p. 241.

Herbet includes *Dix hommes nus dans des rochers*, the workmanship of which seems to us unlike Domenico's. He attributes two etchings to Domenico. The attribution of one was already suggested by Brulliot; it is a curious composition that Panofsky has since identified as *Pandora*. It bears two monograms: D.B. and Z.B.M. The other one represents *Phama*. It should be noted that the monogram D.B. appears on no other print by Domenico, who used D.F. We see nothing in the technique or style of these etchings to justify attributing them to Domenico. Moreover, we believe they did not originate in Fontainebleau at all but are Italian. As far as one can say, Domenico never used an etching-needle. Mariette's tentative attribution of *Une Femme debout* after Parmigianino is also retained by Herbet, but we have not been able to discover the piece in the Bibliothèque Nationale, where Herbet locates it.

On the other hand, Herbet rejected the attribution of a beautiful print of Rosso's *Sainte Famille*; we are not certain he was right, but the absence of a monogram lends weight to his decision. We suggest attributing to the master a *Vierge à l'enfant* which bears no mark; since the one known proof is cut, it is not impossible that it was originally marked. The workmanship strikes us as Domenico's and shows that particularity which is very rare in engraving and constant with Domenico: *pentimenti*. The admirable draughtsmanship of this *Vierge* implies a famous name as its author and appears to us compatible with the rest of the Florentine's œuvre.

His complete name is Domenico Ricoveri del Barbiere. The earliest document which mentions him is in the Fontainebleau accounts, but it is thought that he was established at Troyes for a long time, perhaps before Rosso's arrival in France. From 1539 until 1565 he travelled between Troyes, where he maintained his residence, and Fontainebleau. His work as a sculptor would require a special study. One can form an idea of his talent from a few documented works such as some portions of the dismembered tomb of Charles de Lorraine at Joinville. His influence on the sculpture of Troyes was all-pervading.[1]

It is the engravings which provide the surest witness of his art. They are infinitely more vivid than those by Pierre Milan. The work is more varied and dynamic, the cut more elastic. Domenico does not hesitate to make corrections; they are particularly visible in his *Gloria* (hair, chin and left shoulder). He has a profound sense of modelling, as one would expect of a sculptor. Above all, he is an artist.

Two delicate questions arise: the date of his engravings and the origin of their compositions. As for the second, one notices straightaway that in the three cases where it can be shown that Domenico reproduced someone else's work – the two portions of Michelangelo's *Last Judgment* (Pls DB 3, 4) and Primaticcio's *Banquet d'Alexandre* (Pl. DB 7) in the chamber of Mme d'Etampes – Domenico scrupulously indicated his source. This leads us to wonder whether the rest are not of his own invention, or at least a free adaptation of borrowed subjects. This could be the case, for example, with the plate of *Ecorchés et squelettes* which seems to us to reflect something of the book on anatomy planned by Rosso, but which is not necessarily the engraving of a drawing by that master and perhaps rather a personal adaptation of figures borrowed from different drawings. Despite Rosso's evident influence, plates like *Cléopâtre* (Pl. DB 8) or *Amphiarao* (Pl. DB 6) do not seem to us his compositions. If Domenico invented them himself, then he must be recognized as an artist of the first rank.

---

[1] On this subject, see Raymond Kœchlin and J.-J. Marquet de Vasselot, *La Sculpture à Troyes et dans la Champagne méridionale au XVIe siècle*, Paris 1900; and for the documents concerning Domenico del Barbiere see the old study by Babeau, 'Dominique Florentin, sculpteur du XVIe siècle', *Réunion des Sociétés des Beaux Arts des Départments*, 1877, pp. 108-41.

As for the dates, there are hardly any guides. The two engravings after *The Last Judgment*, which was finished in 1541, must be later than that year. We have seen that the compositions for Mme d'Etampes' chamber, of which the *Banquet d'Alexandre* was one, are among those most frequently represented by the etchers around 1544-46, when they had just been completed. One may presume that Domenico's engraving is of the same period. Other plates may be earlier, some later: we would say only that the homogeneity of this engraved œuvre makes us believe that it does not extend over a long period. Our intuition – and it is no more than that – would be to place this period around 1540-45, the same time as Pierre Milan and the etchers.

It seems to us probable, but not certain, that Domenico's prints were executed at Fontainebleau. It is improbable that they were done at Troyes, but they could have been executed in Paris. Nor can we say whether he appeared as a technical innovator or followed the vogue. In fine, the earliest date we find is inscribed by Master L.D. on a print in 1540. Did he learn engraving from Pierre Milan or Domenico, or in fact was it he, having learned the art elsewhere, who taught it to them? Nothing permits us to say – nor whether L.D.'s engravings were executed at Fontainebleau. At least this date is valuable because it is earlier than all the etchings we know. In these circumstances, ought we to attribute a rôle to the engraver Jean Viset, whose presence was noted at Fontainebleau in 1536 in a document analysed earlier? Nothing is less certain in the absence of any information about the work of Viset. One observation, however, may be useful: Domenico, L.D. and Milan, in spite of great differences, have quite a lot in common in their use of the burin, their application of broad elastic cuts, simply crossed, generally on the oblique and with a very luminous effect. We see this in only one predecessor, Caraglio, and precisely in his interpretations of Rosso. Thus the possibility is not excluded that the great painter may have some direct responsibility for the rise of engraving in France and may have encouraged it before his death.

One ought to show in conclusion how prints contributed to the diffusion of the art of the School of Fontainebleau. But in order to answer this question precisely, to say how printmaking propagated certain themes and certain motifs, and to what point it had a genuinely stylistic influence, to distinguish properly between its impact and that of the direct contact of artists who came to Fontainebleau – this would call for a long and searching enquiry which goes far beyond the framework of this book. One may state in a general way, almost *a priori*, that prints made the compositions of Fontainebleau widely known, but that direct study of the Château's decorations and contact with the artists left deeper traces – on an artist like Martin de Vos, for example. One may also acknowledge, as Y. Metman does, that prints were most effective in the dissemination of the ornamental style. Thus Flemish ornamentation, called the 'Floris style', seems to have developed from Fontainebleau examples. But even in this area there are surprises: on the one hand the significance may change in transmission, and on the other the influences very quickly become reciprocal. When we turn towards Italy, it is sometimes difficult to distinguish between what comes from Fontainebleau and what is a parallel development from the same antecedents. One is reduced to considering individual examples, such as the copies of Fantuzzi's ornamental etchings made by G.B. Pittoni (and not by Schiavone, as was long believed). It is the multiplication of such examples that can tell us more, and above all their analysis; not so much, perhaps, in order to construct an inventory of influences as to appreciate the radical transformations produced through the mechanism of these borrowings. For – it must be said – we are basically very ill informed about what the radiation of an artistic centre signifies.

PLATES

FANTUZZI

F.P. I

A.F. 1

A.F. 1 bis

A.F. 2

A.F. 3

A.F. 4

A.F. 5

A.F. 6

A.F. 7

A.F. 8

A.F. 9

A.F 10

A.F. 11

A.F. 12

A.F. 13

A.F. 14

A.F. 1.

A.F. 16

A.F. 17

A.F. 18

A.F. 19

A.F. 20

A.F. 21

A.F. 22

A.F. 23

A.F. 24

A.F. 25

A.F. 26

A.F. 29

A.F. 30

A.F. 31

A.F. 32

A.F. 33

A.F. 34

A.F. 35

A.F. 36

A.F. 37

A.F. 38

A.F. 39

A.F. 40

A.F. 41

A.F. 42

A.F. 43

A.F. 44

A.F. 45

A.F. 46

A.F. 47

A.F. 48

A.F. 49

A.F. 50

A.F. 51

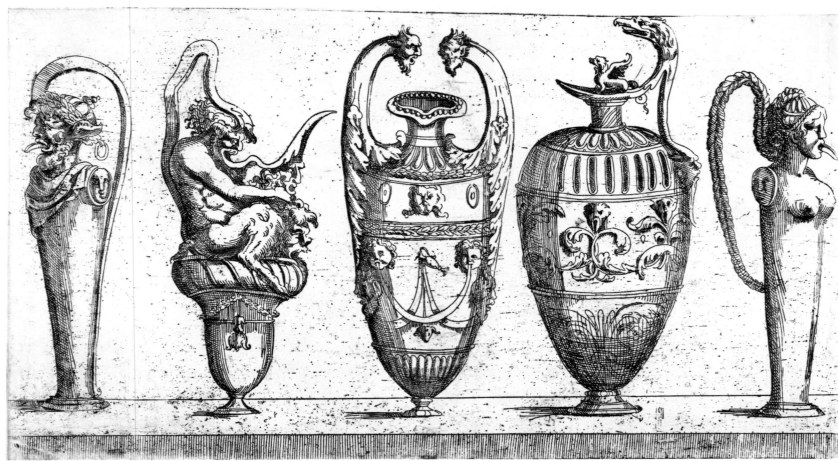

A.F. 52

A.F. 53

A.F. 54 a   A.F. 54 b

A.F. 55

A.F. 56

A.F. 57

D.3159

A.F. 58

A.F. 59

A.F. 60

A.F. 61

A.F. 62

A.F. 63

A.F. 64

A.F. 65

A.F. 66

A.F. 67

A.F. 68

A.F. 69

A.F. 70

A.F. 71

Bologna, Inuento; NF
1544

A.F. 72

A.F. 73

A.F. 75

A.F. 76 a

A.F. 76 b

A.F. 77

A.F. 78

A.F. 79

A.F. 80

A.F. 81

ALCYTOE·CVM·SORORIBVS·IN·VESPERTILIONES·

A.F. 82

A.F. 83

Roma D Latini Inagul.

A.F. 84

A.F. 86

A.F. 87

A.F. 88

A.F. 89

A.F. 90   A.F. 91

A.F. 92

A.F. 93

A.F. 94

A.F. 95

A.F. 96

A.F. 97

A.F. 98

A.F. 99

A.F. 100

A.F. 101

A.F. 102

XII

A.F. 103

A.F. 104

A.F. 105

A.F. 106

A.F. 107

A.F. 108

A.F. 109

A.F. 110

A.F. 111

MASTER L.D.

L.D. 1

L.D. 2

L.D. 3

L.D. 4

L.D. 5

L.D. 6

A·fontaine·bleau

L.D. 7

L.D. 8

L.D. 9

L.D. 10

L.D. 11

L.D. 12

L.D. 13

L.D. 14

L.D. 15

L.D. 16

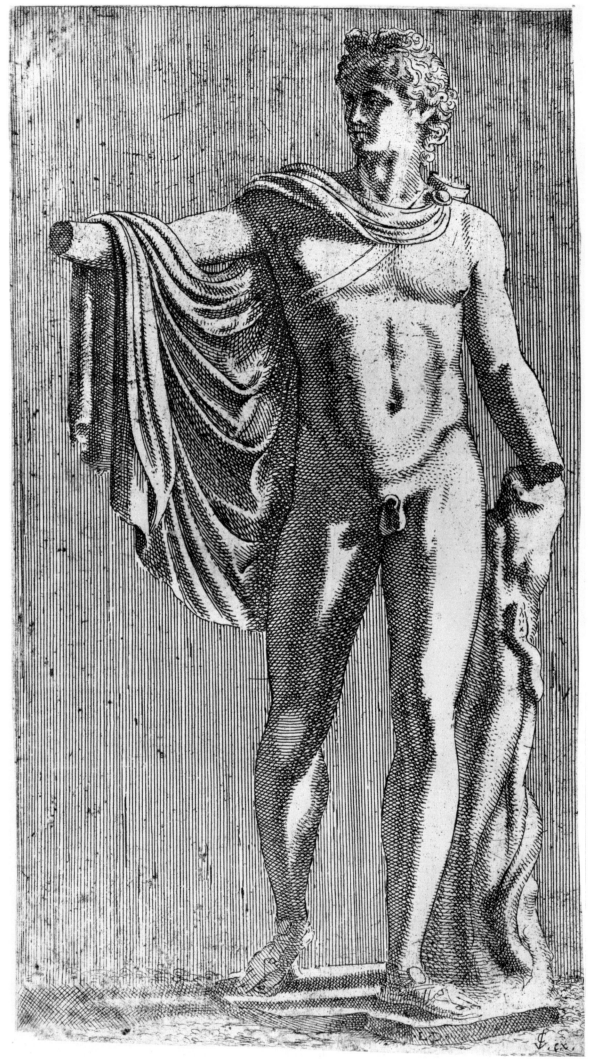

L.D. 17

L.D. 18

L.D. 19

L.D. 20

L.D. 21

L.D. 22

L.D. 23

L.D. 24

Bologna
L. D

Bologna

Bologna

L.D. 27

Calliope

Bologna
L.D.

L.D. 28

Bologna
L.D.

L.D. 30

Bologna

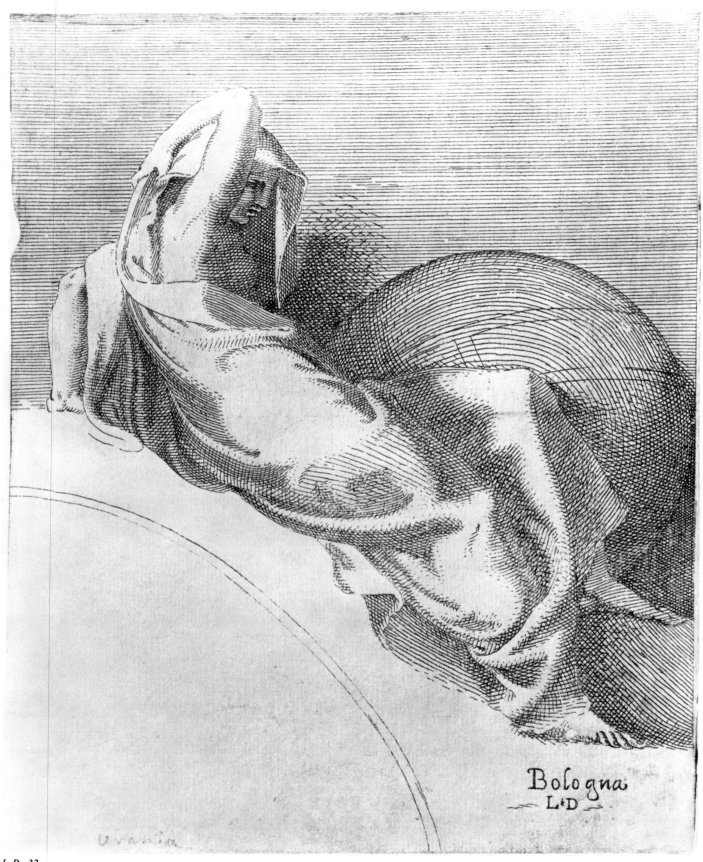

Urania

L.D. 32

Bologna
L.D.

A · fontainebleau

Bologna
L·D

L.D. 34

L.D. 35

L.D. 36

L.D. 39

L.D. 40

L.D. 41

L.D. 42 *detail*

L.D. 42

L.D. 43

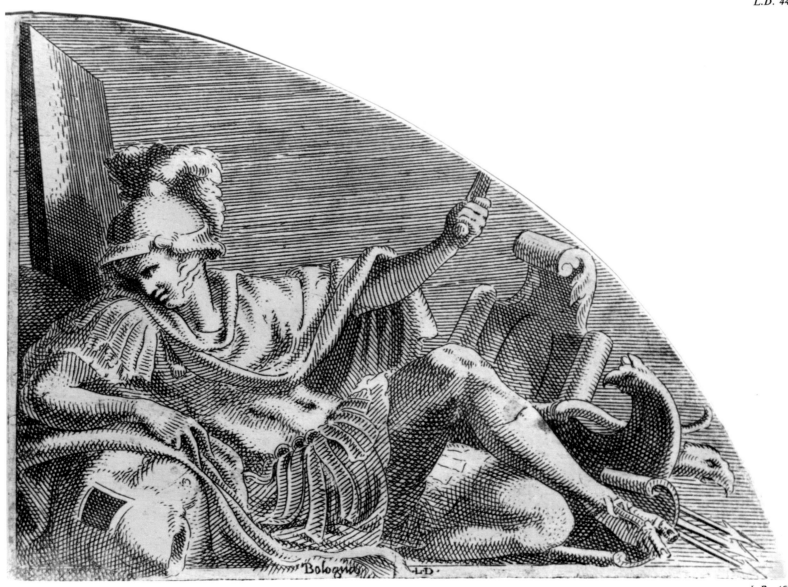

L.D. 46

L.D. 47

L.D. 48

L.D. 49

L.D. 50

L.D. 51

Bologna.

L.D. 52

L.D. 53-54, 55-56

L.D. 55

L.D. 56

L.D. 57

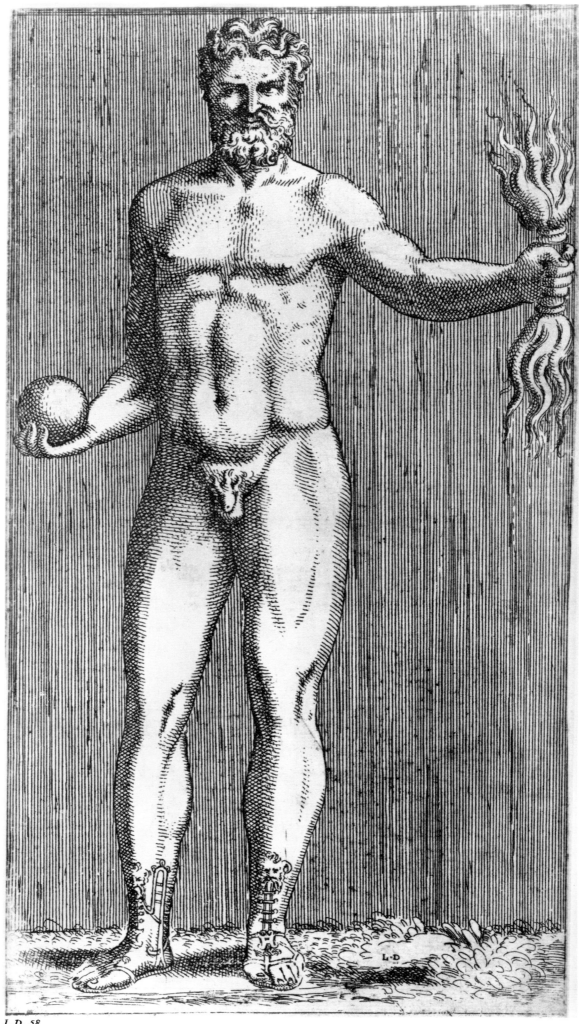

L.D. 58

·Bol· inventeur· à Fonteine bleau·

L.D. 59

L.D. 60

L.D. 61

L.D. 62

L.D. 63

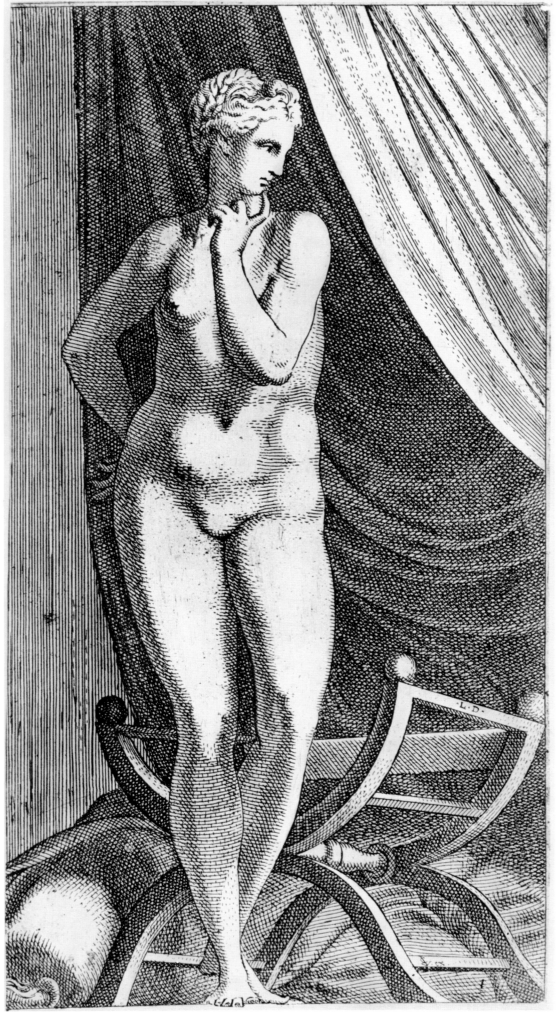

L.D. 64

L.D. 65

L.D. 66

L.D. 67

L.D. 68

L.D. 69

L.D. 70

L.D. 71

L.D. 72

L.D. 73

L.D. 74

L.D. 75

ARBORVM GENERA NVMINIBVS SVIS DICATA
PERPETVO SERVANTVR VT IOVI ÆSCVLVS
APOLLINI LAVRVS MINERVÆ OLEA
VENERI MIRTVS HERCVLI POPVLVS
PLIN LIB XII
1547
LD

·L·D· ·1547·

L.D. 77

·L·D·∴·1547·

L.D. 78

L.D. 79

L.D. 80

L.D. 81

L.D. 82

L.D. 83

L.D. 84

SVB · PENNIS · EIVS · TVTVS · ERO ·
· L · PENNIS · R

L.D. 85

SVB · PENNIS · EIVS · TVTVS · ERO ·
· L · PENNIS · R ·

L.D. 85 bis

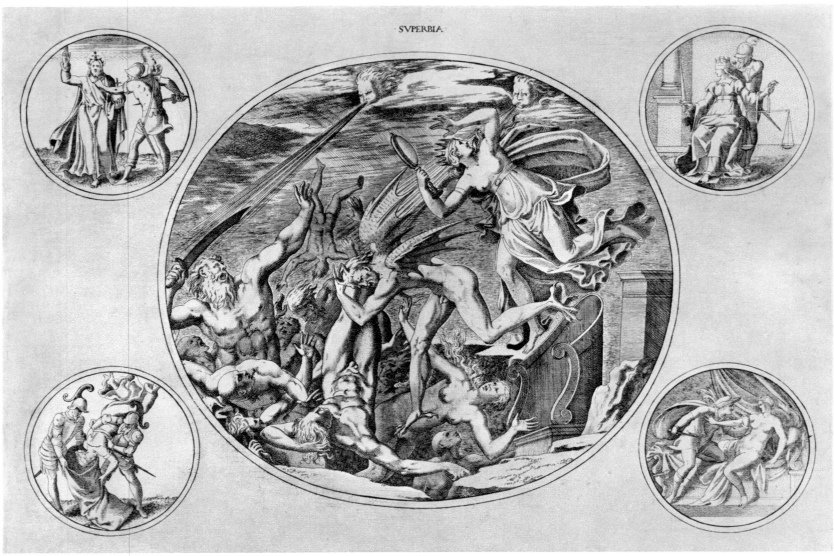

SVPERBIA

L.D. 86

AVARITIA

L.D. 87

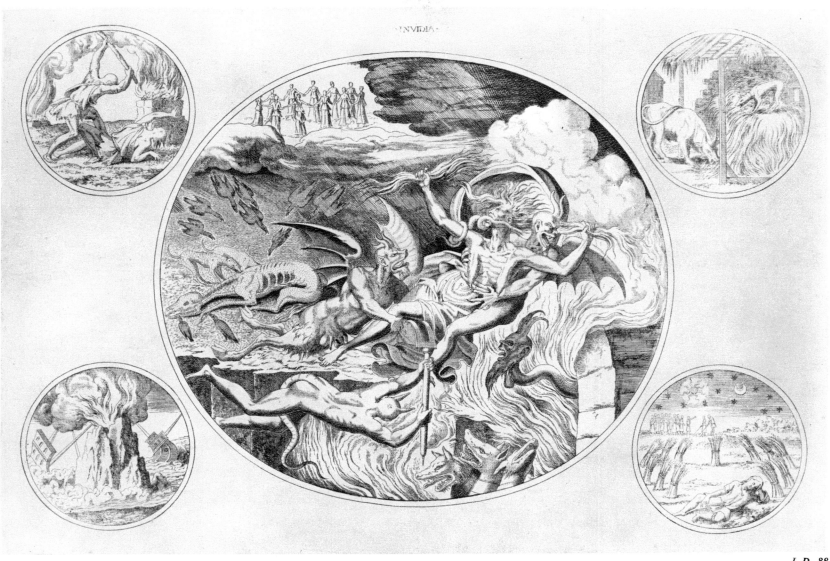

·IRA·

L.D. 90

LVSSVRIA

L.D. 91

PYGRITIA

L.D. 92

Cum priuilegio Regis:~

L.D. 93

Deuaſtat ſiculos frugum dea funditus agros

L.D. 94

L.D. 95

Femme de l'Isle   *de Chio.*

Villageois Grec

L.D. 97

Cadilefquer

L.D. 98

JEAN MIGNON

1543

J.M. 1

J.M. 2

J.M. 3

J.M. 4

Inconu

J.M. 5

J.M. 6

J.M. 7

Io. MIGON.

J.M. 8

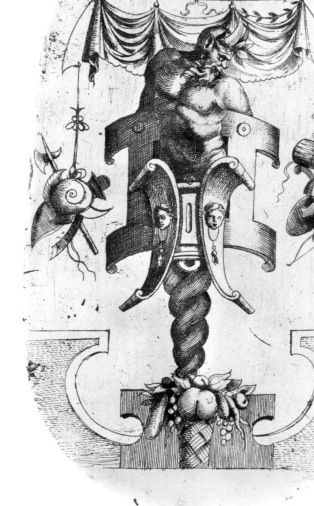

J.M. 9   J.M. 10

J.M. 11

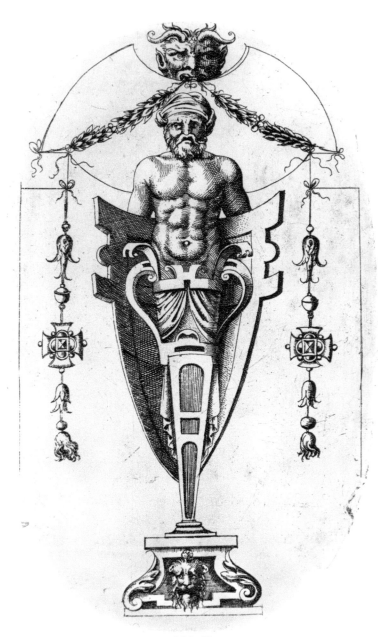

J.M. 12

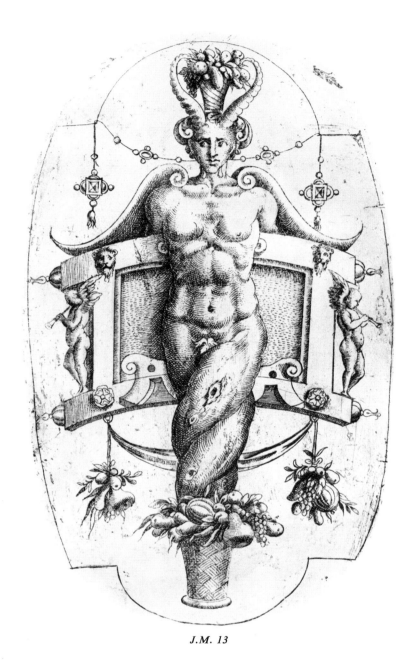

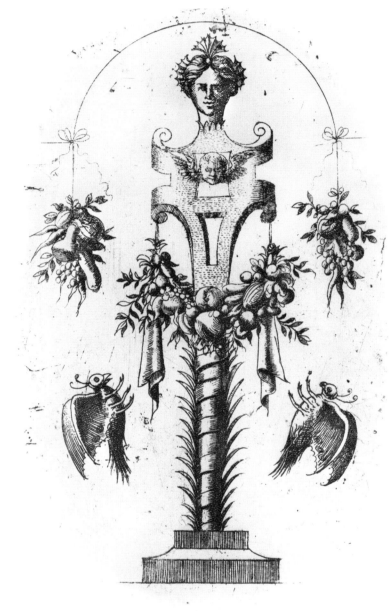

J.M. 13   J.M. 14

J.M. 15

J.M. 16

J.M. 17

J.M. 18

J.M. 19

J.M. 20

J.M. 21

J.M. 22

J.M. 23

J.M. 24

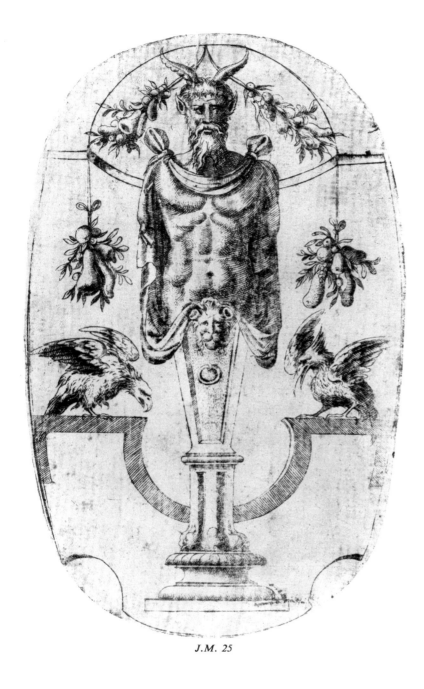

J.M. 25   J.M. 26

J.M. 27

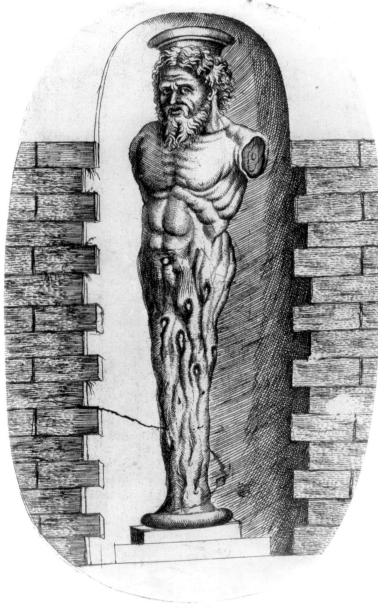

J.M. 28

J.M. 29

J.M. 30

J.M. 32

J.M. 34

J.M. 35

J.M. 36

J.M. 37

J.M. 38

J.M. 39

J.M. 46

J.M. 47

J.M. 48

J.M. 49

J.M. 51

EGO SVM RESVRRECTIO
ET VITA

VENITE
BENEDICTI
PATRIS
MEI

ITE
MALEDICTI
IN IGNEM
ETERNVM

OPERA EORVM
SEQVVNTVR ILLOS

J.M. 53

PLACVIT
DEVM
OBEDIENTIA

J.M. 54

J.M. 55 b

J.M. 55 a

J.M. 58

J.M. 59 a

J.M. 59 b

DOMINVM
COGNOSCITE
VESTRVM

J.M. 60

GEOFFROY DUMOÛTIER

y Dumoustier fecit

G.D. 1

G.D. 2

G.D. 3

Geofroy Dumoutier fecit

G.D. 4

G.D. 5

G.D. 6

G.D. 7

G.D. 8

G.D. 9

G.D. 10

G.D. 11

Si aulcun a peche nous auons vng aduocat au prez du pere Ihc crist
Le iuste et cestuy est La reconciliation pour noz peschez

1 Timo. 2

Il est ung Dieu et aussi ung mediateur entre Dieu et Les
homes Lhome Iesuchrist qui a dōne soymesmes redēptiō pour tous

G.D. 13

Geofroy Dumonstier f.

G.D. 14

Nous ne prefchons point nousmesmes
mais Iesuchrist nostre seigneur.
2 corin 4

Certes nous ne sommes point comme plusieurs
faisans marchandise de la parolle de dieu, mais
nous parlons comme en pureté comme de par
dieu deuant dieu par Christ   2 corin 2

G.D. 15

G.D. 16

G.D. 17

Aug: Quirmeüer fecit

G.D. 18

G.D. 19

geffroy Dumonstier fecit

G.D. 20

G.D. 21

G.D. 22

Geffroy Dumonstier f.
1547.

G.D. 23

G.D. 24

Geoffroy Dumonstier. f.

Geoffroy Dumonstier fecit

G.D. 25   G.D. 26

LÉONARD LIMOSIN

L.L. 2

LEONARD
LIMOSIN 1544

L.L. 4

L.L. 5

LEONARD
LIMOSIN

L.L. 6

LEONARD
LIMOSIN

L.L. 7

L.L. 8

THE SUPPOSED JUSTE DE JUSTE

J. 1

J. 2

J. 3

J. 4

J. 5

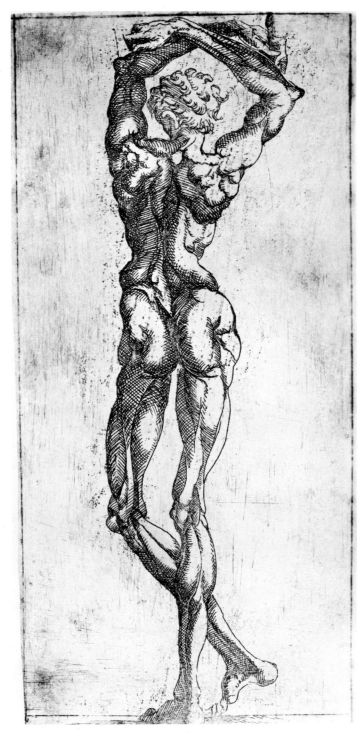

J. 6   J. 7

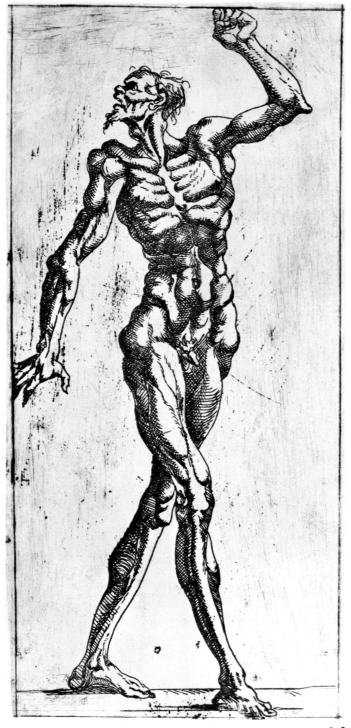

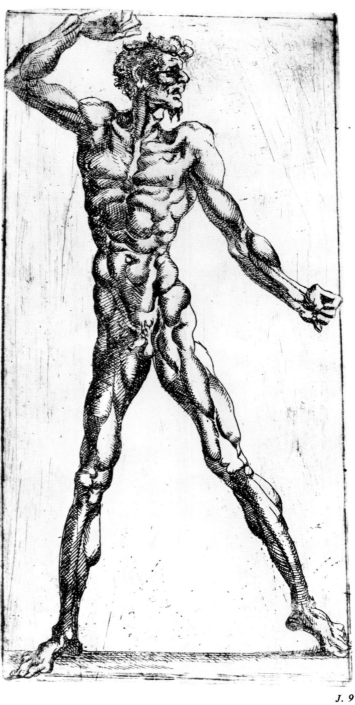

J. 8

J. 9

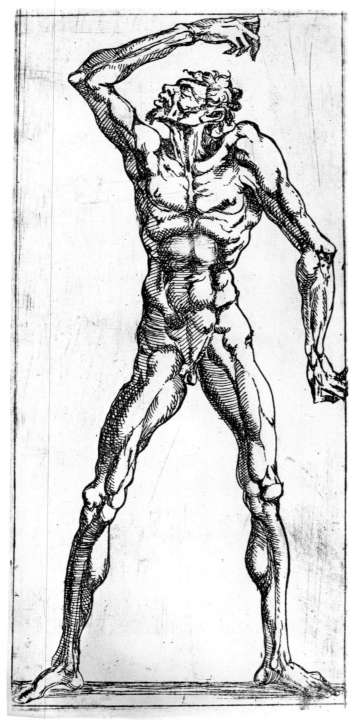

J. 10

J. 11

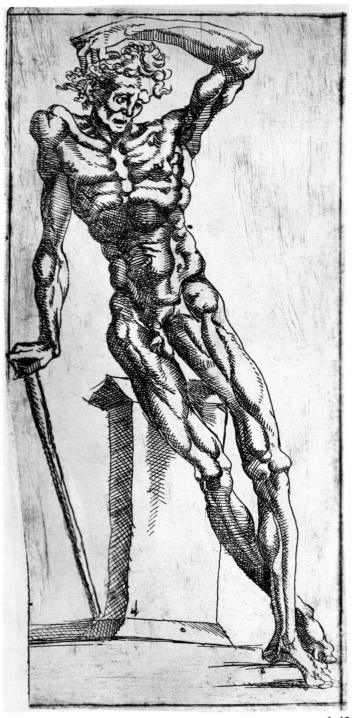

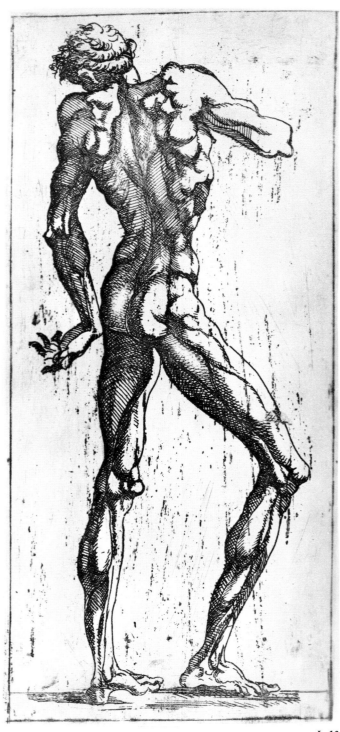

J. 12

J. 13

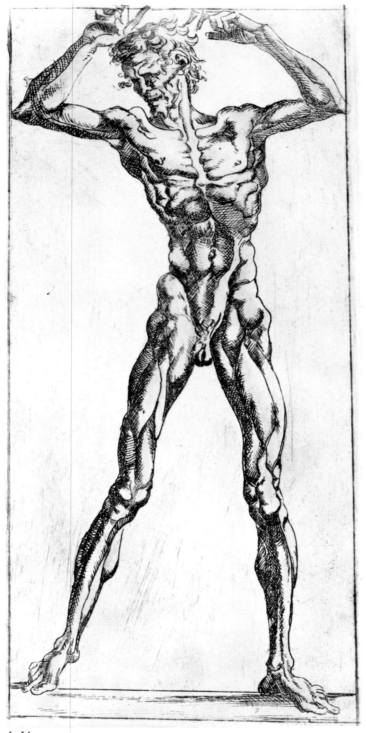

J. 14

J. 15

J. 16

J. 17

PIERRE MILAN

P.M. 2

Rous·de·Rous·Floren·Inuentor:

P.M. 3

P.M. 4

Iulius Romanus Inuentor

P.M. 6

O Phidias, o Apelles, Quidquamne ornatius vestris temporibus excogitari potuit, ea sculptura, cuius hic picturam cernitis, Quam
Franciscus primus, Francorum Rex potentiss bonarum artium ac literarum pater, sub Diana, à venatu conquiescentis,
atque vrnam Fontisbellaquæ effundentis statua, Domi suæ inchoatam reliquit.

Cum priuilegio Regis.   Rous. Floren. Inuen.

P.M. 7 detail

DOMENICO DEL BARBIERE

D.B. 2

MICHELANGIOLO·INVNTRE·INROMA·
NELA·CHAPELA·DELPAPA·

DOMENICO·
FIORENTINO

D.B. 3

D.B. 4

D.B. 5

AMPHIARAO

DOMENICO DELBARBIER·

D.B. 7

D.B. 8

GLORIA·

DOMENICO·
DELBARBIERE·
FIORNTINO·

D.B. 9

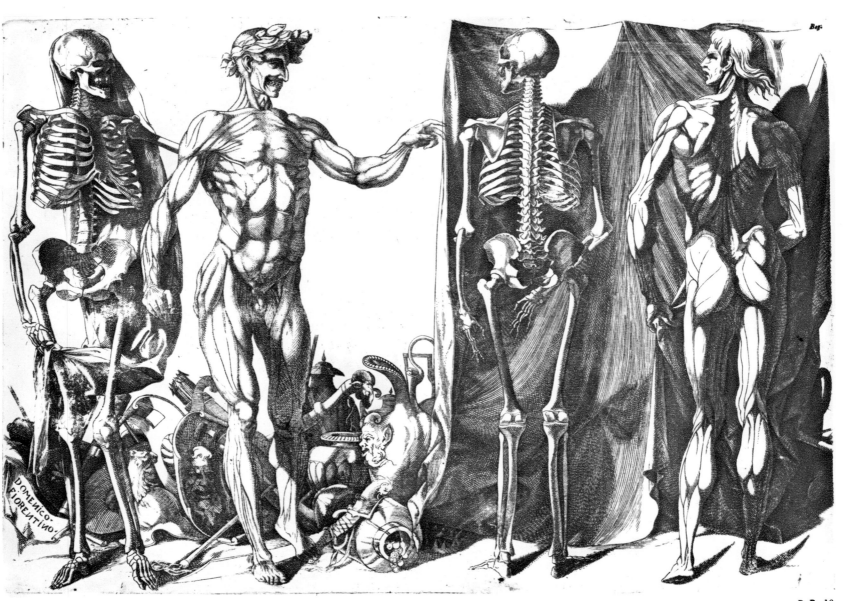

D.B. 11

D.B. 12

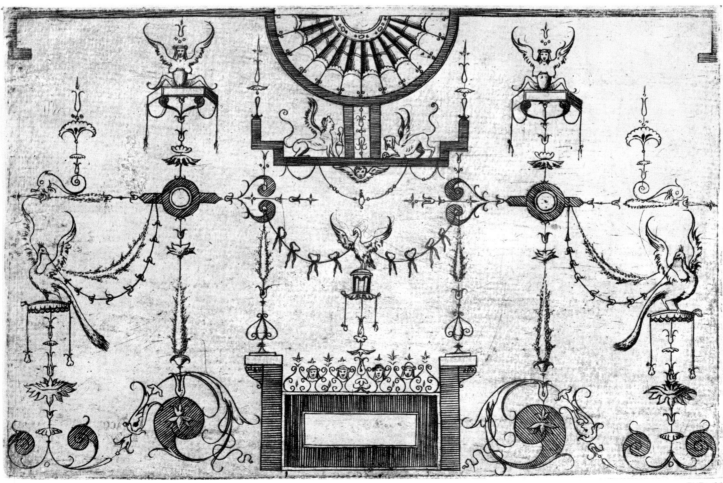

D.B. 13

D.B. 14

D.B. 15

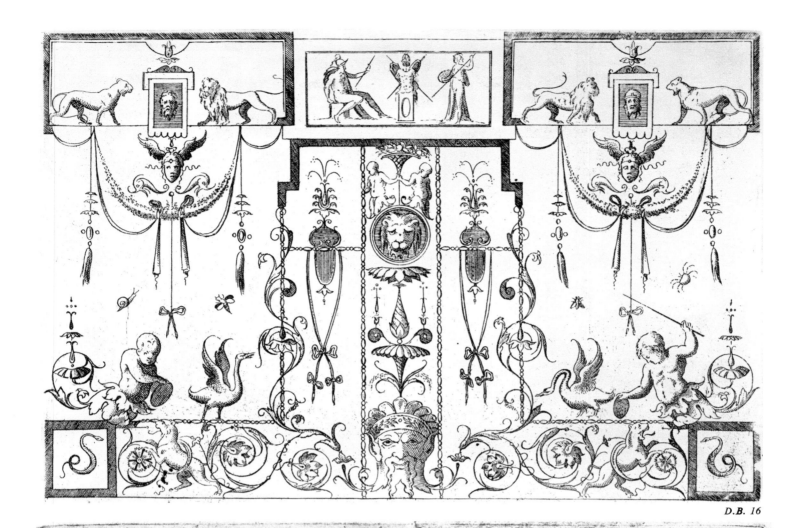

D.B. 16

D.B. 17

D.B. 18

D.B. 19

D.B. 20

D.B. 21

D.B. 22

TABLE OF CONCORDANCES

INDEX OF PLATES BY SUBJECT

SOURCES OF THE PLATES

TABLE OF CONCORDANCES

Key: H.   *refers to Herbet's catalogues;*
R.D.   *refers to Robert-Dumesnil's catalogues;*
Z.   *refers to plates reproduced in this book;*
Rej.   *signifies that we have rejected the piece from the œuvre of the artist in question; when it appears in this book under another name, we have replaced this sign with the artist's initial and the plate number;*
n.t.   *means that we have been unable to find copies.*

FANTUZZI

H.	Z.	H.	Z.
1	33	54	68
2	34	55	75
3	35	56	50
4	36	57	58
5	37	58	1
6	44	59	14
7	60	60	13
8	51	61	57
9	41	62	62
10	79	63	10
11	45	64	Rej.
12	49	65	63
13	39	66	11
14	40	67	12
15	61	68	15
16	Rej.	69	Rej.
17	78	70	3
18	55	71	4
19	46	72	5
20	47	73	6
21	48	74	7
22	83	75	8
23	54	76	18
24	52	77	76
25	53	78	59
26	32	79	77
27	23	80	Rej.
28	24	81	Rej.
29	25	82	Rej.
30	Rej.	83	n.t.
31	28	84	19
32	29	85	101
33	Rej.	86	85
34	26	87	109
35	27	88	98
36	31	89	108
37	38	90	110
38	74	91	96
39	56	92	87
40	20	93	102
41	21	94	86
42	Rej.	95	89
43	n.t.	96	88
44	72	97	95
45	17	98	97
46	Rej.	99	107
47	83	100	92
48	70	101	84
49	Rej.	102	104
50	69	103	111
51	71	104	105
52	81	105	106
53	73	106	30

MASTER L.D.

H.	Z.	H.	Z.	H.	Z.
1	46	49	5	127	97
2	9	50	61	128	98
3	10	51	4	163	94
4	8	52	48	184	95
5	11	53	21	227	40
6	68	54	Rej.	228	41
7	15	55	14		
8	81	56	62		
9	82	57	39		
10	49	58	93		
11	6	59	A.F.64		
12	50	60	★		
13	51	61	70		
14	67	62	77		
15	59	63	78		
16	7	64	79		
17	60	65	85		
18	43	66	86		
19	25	67	87		
20	26	68	91		
21	27	69	88		
22	28	70	89		
23	29	71	90		
24	30	72	92		
25	31	73	74		
26	32	74	71		
27	33	75	J.M.42		
28	34	76	73		
29	35	77	53		
30	36	78	54		
31	44	79	55		
32	45	80	56		
33	37	81	47		
34	13	82	2		
35	23	83	Rej.		
36	66	84	1		
37	52	85	57		
38	38	86	63		
39	J.M.54	87	3		
40	84	88	20		
41	Rej.	89	83		
42	75	90	58		
43	24	91	17		
44	65	92	80		
45	64	93	19		
46	76	94	18		
47	12	95	A.F.92?		
48	16	100	96		

JEAN MIGNON

H.	Z.
1	56
2	57
3	39
4	49
5	Rej.
6	29
7	Rej.
8	30
9	50
10	55
11	31
12	41
13	45
14	44
15	43
16	48
17	38
18	Rej.
19	53
20	34
21	40
22	60
23	46
24	8
25	7
26	4
27	52

★ *Late work not reproduced here, like most of the numbers above 95; cf. pp. 23-24 of the Introduction.*

DUMOÛTIER

R.D.	Z.
1	1a
2	1b
3	2
4	3
5	4
6	5
7	7
8	10
9	18

H.	Z.
10	11
11	13
12	12
13	14
14	21
15	22
16	17
17	24
18	23
19	25
20	26
21	19
22	20

Supplement

1	6
2	9
3	15
4	16

LÉONARD LIMOSIN

H.	Z.
1	1
2	2
3	3
4	4
5	5
6	5
7	6
8	8

JUSTE DE JUSTE

H.	Z.
1	1
2	2
3	3
4	4
5	5

DOMENICO DEL BARBIERE

H.	Z.
1	2
2	3
3	4
4	5
5	6
6	7
7	9
8	10
9	11
10	n.t.
11	n.t.
12	8
13	Rej.
14	Rej.
15	Rej.
16	12
17	13
18	14
19	15
20	16
21	17
22	18
23	19
24	20
25	21
26	22
27	n.t.

Prints described by Herbet as anonymous etchings which are given attributions here.

8	A.F.65
10	J.M.2
16	J.M.1
17	J.M.5
18	D.B.1
23	J.M.3
28	A.F.66
39	J.M.32
45	A.F.76b
53	J.M.37
68	J.M.33
69	J.M.51
97	A.F.42
99	J.M.59a
100	J.M.59b
106	J.M.58
117	J.M.36
122	A.F.80
126	A.F.43
127	J.M.35

INDEX OF PLATES BY SUBJECT

THE BIBLE

L'Éternel assis sur le globe du monde: AF 64
Création d'Ève: JM 56
Tentation d'Ève: JM 57
Abraham sacrifiant Isaac: JM 54
Rébecca et Eliézer: LD 23
Joseph faisant fouiller les bagages de ses frères
   (?): LD 59
Fin de la stérilité de sainte Anne: GD 1a
Naissance de la Vierge: GD 1b
Présentation de la Vierge: JM 47
L'Annonciation: LL 1
La Visitation: GD 2
La Nativité: AF 65, GD 3–7, LL 2
Sainte Famille: AF 74, JM 1, 3, 4, 5
Adoration des bergers: JM 2
Adoration des mages: JM 39, 49
Jésus prêchant parmi les disciples: GD 8
Jésus guérissant dix lépreux: LD 63
Entrée à Jérusalem: LL 3
Jésus lavant les pieds des disciples: AF 62
La Cène: LL 4
Christ au jardin des Oliviers: LL 5
Arrestation du Christ: LL 6
Jésus renvoyé par Hérode: LL 7
Le portement de Croix: JM 29
Évanouissement de la Vierge: GD 10
Déposition: GD 9
Pietà: AF 66, JM 30
Christ aux limbes: LD 84
La Résurrection: LL 8
Les Saintes femmes allant au Sépulcre: GD 19
Jugement dernier: JM 52, DB 3–4

THE VIRGIN AND SAINTS

La Vierge: GD 12–13, DB 1
L'Immaculée conception: GD 18
Sacrée conversation: LD 57
Mort de la Vierge (incorrect): GD 10
Les Apôtres contemplant le Christ et la Vierge:
   LD 53–56
Saint Jean prêchant au désert: JM 55
Saint Jean à Pathmos: GD 11
Saint Paul: GD 15, 21 (?)
Saint Étienne lapidé: DB 2
Sainte Madeleine transportée au ciel: LD 73
Saints et saintes non identifiés: GD 14, 16–17

ANCIENT HISTORY

Zaleucus se faisant crever un œil: AF 11
Alexandre domptant Bucéphale: LD 50
Apelle peignant Alexandre et Campaspe:
   LD 51
Timoclée devant Alexandre: LD 52
Banquet d'Alexandre: DB 7
Combat des Horaces et des Curiaces (incorrect):
   AF 13
Tarquin et Lucrèce: LD 71
Clélie traversant le fleuve: PM 6

Marcus Curtius se précipitant dans un gouffre:
   JM 48
Camille arrivant au camp des Romains: LD 75
Régulus dans le tonneau: AF 14
Scipion, Banquet de . . .: AF 57, Continence de
   . . .: AF 58, Clémence de . . .: AF 1
César faisant brûler les lettres de Pompée:
   AF 63
L'Empereur Marc-Antoine offrant un sacrifice:
   LD 39
Cléopâtre: LD 24, JM 31, DB 8
Vercingétorix (monument à) (?) AF 29
Triomphe de Sigismond (incorrect): AF 2–9

MYTHOLOGY AND LEGEND

Jupiter: LD 58, entouré des autres divinités:
   LD 76, PM 5
Jupiter envoyant les trois déesses au jugement de
   Pâris: AF 55
Jupiter pressant les nuées: LD 6
Jupiter et Antiope: AF 71, LD 49
Jupiter et Danaë: LD 8
Jupiter enlevant Europe: LD 43
Jupiter et Calisto: PM 4
Jupiter et Sémélé: LD 11, 68
Juno: LD 25
Vénus: LD 26; avec les nymphes au bain: AF
   59, JM 34; avec Mars et l'Amour: AF 68,
   LD 72, JM 38, DB 5; dans la forge de
   Vulcain: LD 67
Mars: LD 45; avec Vénus au bain: AF 68;
   avec Vénus servi à table: LD 74
Apollon: LD 17 (du Belvédère); avec
   Marsyas: AF 76
Diane au repos: LD 13; chassant un cerf:
   LD 78
Mercure enseignant les arts: LD 22
Minerve: AF 105, LD 27
Dispute de Minerve et de Neptune: AF 32
L'Amour tirant des flèches au cœur d'Apollon
   (incorrect): LD 4; les yeux bandés: LD 5
Eros et Antéros: LD 21
Pluton enlevant Proserpine: JM 32
Sur la malédiction de Cérès un des bœufs qui
   trainent une charrue tombe à genoux: LD 94
Saturne endormi (?): AF 72
Hygie: AF 106, 109
Bellone: LD 44
Cybèle: AF 85
Silène porté par deux bacchants: AF 56
Le Jardin de Vertumne: LD 7
Vertumne et Pomone: AF 38
Les Muses: LD 28–36; au pied du Parnasse:
   AF 20; Melpomène: AF 91, 100, 102;
   Euterpe: AF 101
Hercule et Antée: AF 67; couché auprès
   d'Omphale: LD 9; se laissant habiller en
   femme: AF 17, LD 10; combattant de dessus
   le vaisseau des Argonautes: LD 46
La Chute de Phaëton: AF 83; JM 37
Actéon métamorphosé en cerf: JM 60; déchiré
   par ses chiens: LD 38

Adonis poursuivant le sanglier de Calydon:
    LD 77
Mort d'Adonis: AF 27, LD 70, JM 53
Amymone enlevée par un satyre: LD 95
Philémon et Baucis (?): LD 66
Pandore: AF 22
Psyché: LD 1, 2
Une Sybille: AF 73
Les Parques: PM 2, 3
Danse des dryades: PM 1
Danse de faunes et de bacchantes: LD 83
Sujets satyriques: Satyre violentant une
    femme: AF 19; *Nymphe mutilant un satyre:*
    LD 15; *Femme portée vers un satyre:* LD
    81; *Satyre porté vers une femme:* LD 82
Nymphes: Nymphes dans un paysage: LD 12;
    Nymphe regardant un héron s'envoler: LD
    37; *La nymphe de Fontainebleau:* PM 7
Les Filles de Minée: AF 81
Pygmalion sculptant Galatée: LD 48
Jason: AF 77; *labourant le champ:* AF 69;
    tuant le dragon: LD 16
Amphiaraus: DB 6
Méléagre apporte à Atalante le hure du
    sanglier: AF 75
Combat des amazones: LD 80
Jugement de Pâris: JM 40
Jugement de Pâris: JM 80
Enlèvement d'Hélène: JM 41
Bataille sous Troie: JM 42
Achille faisant ses adieux à la fille de Lycomède
    (?): AF 70; *retirant du combat le corps de*
    Patrocle: LD 47
Priam payant la rançon d'Hector (?) JM 8
Le Perfide Sinon introduit par les bergers:
    JM 43
Les Troyens introduisent le cheval de bois:
    JM 44
Pillage de Troie: JM 45
Circé donnant à boire aux compagnons
    d'Ulysse: AF 18, LD 20
Vengeance de Nauplius: AF 26
Entellus et Darès: JM 51

ALLEGORY

L'Église: GD 22
La Charité: JM 6
La Justice: LD 85, GD 25
Les Péchés capitaux: LD 85–92
La Discorde: GD 26
L'Éloquence: GD 24
Le Sacrifice: AF 23
L'Ignorance vaincue: AF 24
L'Unité de l'État: AF 28
L'Éléphant fleurdelysé: AF 25
La Danse: LD 4
La Gloire: DB 9

SUBJECTS OF FANTASY OR GENRE AND ISOLATED FIGURES

Deux femmes romaines: FP unique
Malade auquel on applique des ventouses:
    AF 10
Prisonniers soumis à des supplices: AF 12
Combat de gladiateurs: AF 13
Une Bataille: AF 15
Jeune femme habillée à l'antique avec deux
    enfants: LD 3
Enfants tenant des avirons: LD 40–41
Femme nue debout: LD 64; *Deux femmes nues*
    avec l'Amour: LD 65
Scène de pêche: LD 79
Costumes orientaux: LD 96–98
Combat d'hommes nus: JM 33
Femmes au bain: JM 46
Figures académiques ou gymnastiques: JJ 1–17
Squelettes et écorchés: DB 10
Statues antiques: AF 50, 84–111, LD 17–19,
    61 (?), 62 (?)

ARCHITECTURAL AND DECORATIVE SUBJECTS

Un cryptoportique: AF 82
Cryptoportique de la grotte du Jardin des Pins:
    LD 60
Chapiteau d'ordre composite: LD 69
Termes: JM 9–28
Cariatides: AF 16
Vases: AF 52–54
Ornements avec paysages: AF 33–37, 39, 41,
    43–44, 48–49, 61, JM 36, DB 11
Ornements sans paysage: AF 40, 42, 45–47,
    51, 60, 78–80, JM 7, 35, 58–59, DB 12–22

UNCERTAIN SUBJECTS

Incinération d'un cadavre: AF 21
Personnage tenant une grenade: AF 29
La Fortune faisant boire un prince: AF 30
Jeune homme et jeune femme assis sur un lit:
    AF 70
Un Ange sonnant de la trompe: LD 14
Un Roi agenouillé devant un autel: LD 42
Hommes assemblés autour d'un chameau:
    LD 59
Deux vieillards couverts de manteaux: LD 66
Une femme montrant des taureaux à un homme:
    LD 93
Un vieillard faisant peser le contenu d'un sac
    devant un capitaine: JM 8
Deux hommes en discussion: GD 20
Figure allégorique indéterminée: GD 23

SOURCES OF THE PLATES

PRIMATICCIO

Bibliothèque nationale. Cabinet des Estampes, Paris.

FANTUZZI

Graphische Sammlung Albertina, Vienna: 7, 17, 19, 26, 39, 46, 49, 51, 60, 61, 65, 72, 76a, 98, 101.
Bibliothèque de l'Arsenal, Paris: 37, 50, 82, 96, 99, 104, 105, 106, 108, 109, 110.
Bibliothèque de l'École des Beaux-Arts, Paris: 3, 5, 12, 16, 31, 57, 64, 71, 79, 86, 87, 88, 89, 102.
Bibliothèque nationale. Cabinet des Estampes, Paris: 1, 1 bis, 2, 4, 8, 10, 11, 14, 24, 25, 27, 28, 29, 33, 34, 35, 40, 41, 42, 43, 44, 47, 48, 52, 53, 54a, 54, 55, 56, 58, 63, 66, 67, 68, 69, 73, 74, 75, 76b, 77, 78, 80, 81, 83, 84, 90, 91, 92, 94, 95, 107, 111.
British Museum, London: 6, 9, 13, 21, 22, 23, 36, 38, 45, 59.
Raymond Lewis: 103.
Metropolitan Museum of Art, New York. Rogers Fund 1918: 18.
  Whittelsey Fund 1949: 20, 32, 62, 85, 97.
  Whittelsey Fund 1959: 30.
  Whittelsey Fund 1964: 100.
  Harris Brisbane Dick Fund 1944: 70.
Collection Paul Prouté, Paris: 15.

MASTER L.D.

Graphische Sammlung Albertina, Vienna: 7, 9, 10, 11, 22, 38, 39, 47, 57, 58, 66, 69, 72, 77.
Bibliothèque de l'Arsenal, Paris: 63.
Bibliothèque de l'École des Beaux-Arts, Paris: 2, 13, 14, 15, 23, 24, 30, 32, 33, 35, 36, 40, 41, 43, 44, 45, 61, 67, 68, 70, 71, 73, 76, 80.
Bibliothèque nationale. Cabinet des Estampes, Paris: 3, 4, 5, 6, 8, 16, 17, 18, 19, 20, 21, 25, 26, 27, 28, 29, 31, 34, 46, 48, 49, 51, 53, 54, 55, 56, 59, 60, 62, 64, 65, 74, 75, 78, 79, 81, 82, 85 bis, 93, 94, 95, 96, 97, 98.
British Museum, London: 12, 52, 83.
Metropolitan Museum of Art, New York. Whittelsey Fund 1959: 1, 84.
  Whittelsey Fund 1949: 42.
Museum of Art, Rhode Island School of Design, Providence: 50.
Collection Paul Prouté, Paris: 85, 86, 87, 88, 89, 90, 91, 92.

MIGNON

Graphische Sammlung Albertina, Vienna: 29, 33, 36, 47, 51, 57, 58, 60.
Bibliothèque de l'Arsenal, Paris: 43, 54.

Bibliothèque de l'École des Beaux-Arts, 8, 30, 42, 45, 48, 53, 55b, 56.
Bibliothèque nationale. Cabinet des Estampes, Paris: 2, 3, 4, 23, 24, 25, 26, 27, 28, 32, 35, 37, 38, 39, 46, 49, 50, 52a, 55,
British Museum, London: 1, 5, 6, 34, 52b, 59a, 59b.
Herzog Anton Ulrich Museum, Brunswick: 7.
National Gallery of Art, Washington: 9 – 22.
Collection Paul Prouté, Paris: 31, 40.

DUMOÛTIER

Graphische Sammlung Albertina, Vienna: 24.
Bibliothèque nationale. Cabinet des Estampes, Paris: 1 – 11, 13, 15, 16, 17, 19, 20, 21, 23, 25, 26.
British Museum, London: 22.
Metropolitan Museum of Art. Harris Brisbane Dick Fund 1937: 12, 14, 18.

LIMOSIN

Bibliothèque nationale. Cabinet des Estampes, Paris: 7, 8.
Bibliothèque Royale, Brussels: 2, 5, 6.
Metropolitan Museum of Art. Harris Brisbane Dick Fund 1937: 1, 3, 4.

JUSTE DE JUSTE

Bibliothèque nationale. Cabinet des Estampes, Paris: 1, 2, 4, 6 – 17.
Collection Paul Prouté, Paris: 3, 5.

PIERRE MILAN

Graphische Sammlung Albertina, Vienna: 2, 3, 4.
Bibliotheque de l'École des Beaux-Arts, Paris: 1, 5.
Bibliothèque nationale. Cabinet des Estampes, Paris: 7.
Collection Paul Prouté, Paris: 6.

DOMENICO DEL BARBIERE

Graphische Sammlung Albertina, Vienna: 2, 4, 5, 7, 11.
Bibliothèque de l'Ecole des Beaux-Arts, Paris: 6.
Bibliothèque nationale. Cabinet des Estampes, Paris: 1, 3, 8, 9, 10, 12–22.

DATE DUE

PRIMATICCIO

Unique DEUX FEMMES ROMAINES (TWO ROMAN WOMEN). 195 × 112cm.
This etching is traditionally attributed to Primaticcio himself. We know of no other piece executed in the same style, which is very free and vivid. The drawing is excellent; it may be that the tradition is well-founded and that Primaticcio himself tried a technique that was in vogue.

FANTUZZI

1 LA CLÉMENCE DE SCIPION (THE CLEMENCY OF SCIPIO). H58 first state. 385 × 487.
The composition is certainly by Giulio Romano, but no other version is known. The proportions and the style make us think that it may be an abandoned subject intended for the tapestry of the Triumphs of Scipio made for François I.

Detail LA CLÉMENCE DE SCIPION. Second state.
Fantuzzi has added a foreground with his monogram and the date 1542. In a third state Fantuzzi's monogram is not very well erased and that of the Master of the monogram of Jesus appears on the side; the plate has been restored.

2–9 Plates after designs by Giulio Romano for the so-called 'Frieze of Sigismond' in the Sala dei Stucchi in the Palazzo del Tè, Mantua. The execution of the stucco is attributed to Primaticcio. We have not indicated the preserved drawings, which do not generally correspond exactly to the prints (cf. F. Hartt, *Giulio Romano*, 1958).

2 CAVALIERS SUIVANT UNE AIGLE (RIDERS FOLLOWING AN EAGLE). H n.d. 252 × 390.
Unmarked. Dated 1542.

3 MARCHE DE TROUPES ARMÉES DE BOUCLIERS (MARCHING TROOPS WITH SHIELDS). H70. 266 × 426.
Unmarked.

4 MARCHE DE FRONDEURS (MARCHING SLINGERS). H71. 266 × 420.
Monogram at bottom right.

5 MARCHE DE LICTEURS (MARCHING LICTORS). H72. 260 × 407.
Unmarked.

6 MARCHE DE SACRIFICATEURS (MARCHING SACRIFICERS). H73. 240 × 400.
The monogram is at bottom left on a stone.

7 CAVALIERS TRAVERSANT UNE RIVIÈRE (RIDERS CROSSING A RIVER). H74. 265 × 415.
Unmarked.

8 MARCHE D'ARMURIERS (PROCESSION OF ARMOURERS). H75. 251 × 403.
Unmarked.

9 CAVALIERS PORTANT DES ARCS ET DES JAVELOTS (RIDERS CARRYING BOWS AND JAVELINS). H n.d. 258 × 408.
Unmarked. 1542?

10 LES VENTOUSES (CUPPING). H63. 237 × 405.
The mark is on the foot of the bed. This composition by Giulio Romano, engraved also by Giorgio Ghisi, is painted in the Loggia della Grotta in the Palazzo del Tè. 1542?

11 ZALEUCUS SE LAISSANT CREVER UN ŒIL (ZALEUCUS HAVING AN EYE TAKEN OUT). H66. 275 × 310.
The monogram is on the upright of Zaleucus' chair. The composition by Giulio Romano is painted on the ceiling of the Sala di Atilio Regolo in the Palazzo del Tè. 1542?

12 PRISONNIERS SOUMIS À DES SUPPLICES (PRISONERS BEING TORTURED). H67. 282 × 420.
Monogram at bottom right. The composition by Giulio Romano is painted on the ceiling of the Sala dei Venti, Palazzo del Tè. 1542–43.

13 COMBAT DE GLADIATEURS (COMBAT OF GLADIATORS). H60. 300 × 437.
Monogram at the angle of the barrier on the left. The composition by Giulio Romano is painted on the ceiling of the Sala dei Venti, Palazzo del Tè. The subject is not, as Herbet says, a combat between the Horatii and the Curiatii.

14 RÉGULUS DANS LE TONNEAU (REGULUS IN THE CASK). H59. 342 × 396.
The monogram is towards the left on the pliers. The composition by Giulio Romano is painted on the ceiling of the Sala di Atilio Regolo, Palazzo del Tè, and two other prints of it exist, one anonymous and the other by Diana Scultori. 1542–43.

15 UNE BATAILLE (A BATTLE). H68. 330 × 460.
Unmarked. Composition by Giulio Romano painted in the Sala di Troia in the ducal palace of Mantua. An original drawing in the Louvre (3,530) provides variants. 1542–43.

16 UN BARBARE ET UNE FEMME À L'ANTIQUE (A BARBARIAN AND A WOMAN IN ANTIQUE STYLE), caryatids. H n.d. 300 × 260.
Unmarked. The attribution causes no doubt. The design is certainly by Giulio Romano but there is no other trace of it. 1542–43.

17 HERCULE SE LAISSANT HABILLER EN FEMME (HERCULES BEING DRESSED AS A WOMAN). H45. 253 × 414.
Unmarked. The composition by Primaticcio is painted in the porch of the Porte Dorée. Original drawing in the Albertina. 1542–43.

18 CIRCÉ DONNANT À BOIRE AUX COMPAGNONS D'ULYSSE (CIRCE GIVING A DRINK TO ULYSSES' COMPANIONS). H76. Diameter 220.
Monogram at bottom right. After Parmiginiano; the original drawing is in the Uffizi, Florence. This composition, also etched by Master L.D. (No. 20), had a great success in prints (three chiaroscuros, and an engraving by Bonasone). A second state bears the superscription 'Aug. Quesnel excud.' above the monogram. Probably 1542.

19 UN SATYRE VIOLENTANT UNE FEMME DÉFENDUE PAR TROIS AMOURS (A SATYR ASSAULTING A WOMAN DEFENDED BY THREE CUPIDS). H84. 393 × 267.
Unmarked. In the proofs we know the etching is very pale, with engraved revisions. We do not know the author of the composition, which makes us think of Salviati. 1542–43.

20 LES MUSES AU PIED DU PARNASSE (THE MUSES AT THE FOOT OF MOUNT PARNASSUS). H40. 250 × 385.
Monogram at bottom right. Kusenberg, perhaps wrongly, rejects Rosso as the author of the composition, and suggests Salviati. One might also consider Primaticcio. Fantuzzi has marked it so strongly with his interpretation that it is difficult to judge. 1542–43.

21 INCINÉRATION D'UN CADAVRE (BURNING OF A CORPSE). H41. 261 × 404.
Monogram at bottom left. Mariette's suggested attribution of the composition to Rosso has never been challenged, but we do not know where it was intended for. A rather weak drawing with indented frame, which omits the figure at bottom right, is at Weimar. A proof of the print in the Bibliothèque Nationale bears the indication 'Sardanaple brulé dans son palais'. 1542–43.

22 PANDORE OUVRANT LA BOÎTE (PANDORA OPENING THE BOX). H n.d. 220 × 281.
Monogram at bottom right. The original drawing of this composition by Rosso is in the Ecole des Beaux-Arts. According to D. and E. Panofsky, this is a case of an abandoned project for the Galerie François I which was replaced by L'Ignorance vaincue (No. 24).

23–37 Prints related to the Galerie François I. We have considered it useful to group all Fantuzzi's prints bearing on the Galerie François I, even though this disturbs the chronological order a little; the first of these date from 1542 and the last probably the end of 1543 or even 1544. As these prints differ sometimes from the executed decorations, we believe that they were, in general, made from preparatory drawings. It is also possible that they are linked with the preparation of the tapestries in Vienna.

23 LE SACRIFICE (THE SACRIFICE). H27. 268 × 402.
Herbet was not aware of a first state of this print in which Fantuzzi's monogram is lightly inscribed in drypoint on the riser of the first step; below is the inscription: A FONT. BELEO. 1542 RO. INVE. These marks must have disappeared very quickly. A quite different variant is attributed to Boyvin.

24 L'IGNORANCE VAINCUE (IGNORANCE DEFEATED). H28. 300 × 425.
Unmarked. 1542?

25 L'ÉLÉPHANT FLEURDELYSÉ (ELEPHANT WITH FLEUR DE LYS). H29. 293 × 428.
The monogram is at far right centre. Panofsky suggests seeing an allegorical representation of François I in this majestic animal which bears his emblems.

26 LA VENGEANCE DE NAUPLIOS (THE REVENGE OF NAUPLIUS). H34. 305 × 434.
Unmarked. 1542–43.

27 LA MORT D'ADONIS (THE DEATH OF ADONIS). H35. 288 × 240.
Unmarked. 1542–43.

28 L'UNITÉ DE L'ÉTAT (THE UNITY OF THE STATE). H31. 286 × 405.
The monogram described by Bartsch is only in ink on the Albertina copy which he described; it is not etched into the plate. Probably 1543.

29 MONUMENT À VERCINGETORIX (MONUMENT TO VERCINGETORIX). H32. 405 × 250.
Unmarked. Variant of the central figure in the preceding subject. It was Panofsky who suggested that this figure is Vercingetorix. 1542–43.

30 LA FORTUNE FAISANT BOIRE UN PRINCE (FORTUNE MAKING A PRINCE DRINK). H106. Diameter 218. Monogram at bottom. This is the composition of a stucco medallion on the west wall of the Gallery, at the right of the door. The subject escapes us. Probably 1543.

31 COMBAT DES CENTAURES ET DES LAPITHES (COMBAT OF CENTAURS AND LAPITHS). H36. Diameter 300.
Unmarked. The composition is very different from

the one painted in the Galerie, but perhaps it is a preliminary study. 1543–44.

32 LA DISPUTE DE MINERVE ET DE NEPTUNE (THE DISPUTE BETWEEN MINERVA AND NEPTUNE). H26. 260 × 417.
Unmarked. No one contests the attribution of this composition to Rosso. There is another print of it attributed to Boyvin. It is not certain that the subject figured originally above the west door, where it was painted in the nineteenth century, probably by Alaux, after the print. 1542–43.

33 ENCADREMENT DE L'IGNORANCE VAINCUE (FRAME OF IGNORANCE DEFEATED). H1. 265 × 533.
Monogram at bottom left, dated 1543.

34 ENCADREMENT DE LA DESTRUCTION DE CATANE (FRAME OF THE DESTRUCTION OF CATANIA). H2. 243 × 495.
Bartsch and Herbet refer to a monogram at bottom left which we have not been able to find. 1542–43.

35 ENCADREMENT DE DANAÉ (FRAME OF DANAÉ). H3. 260 × 535.
The monogram is at bottom left. The same frame is found around the *Nymphe de Fontainebleau*, engraved by P. Milan and finished by Boyvin with subjects in the two small medallions which are left empty here. Probably 1543.

36 ENCADREMENT DE VENUS CHÂTIANT L'AMOUR (FRAME OF VENUS PUNISHING CUPID). H4. 244 × 497.
Monogram at bottom left. Probably 1543.

37 ENCADREMENT DU COMBAT DES CENTAURES ET DES LAPITHES (FRAME OF COMBAT OF CENTAURS AND LAPITHS). H5. 334 × 516.
Monogram at bottom right. 1542–43.

38–39 DÉCORATION DU PAVILLON DE POMONE (DECORATION OF THE PAVILION OF POMONA).
These two prints of Rosso's invention preserve the memory of a pavilion which was in the corner of the Jardin des Pins at Fontainebleau and was demolished. It contained two frescoes, one by Rosso etched by Fantuzzi, and one by Primaticcio which is our L.D.7. According to Mariette, the stuccos etched by Fantuzzi were the same for both compositions.

38 VERTUMNE ET POMONE (VERTUMNUS AND POMONA). H37. 348 × 347.
Monogram at bottom left. The Louvre has a drawing attributed to Rosso himself; though this is generally accepted, we find it doubtful. 1542–43.

39 PAYSAGE DANS LES ORNEMENTS DU PAVILLON DE POMONE (LANDSCAPE WITHIN THE ORNAMENTS OF THE PAVILION OF POMONA) H13. 258 × 410.
Unmarked. 1542–43.

40 ORNEMENTS D'UN PLAFOND (ORNAMENTATION OF A CEILING). H14. 374 × 244.
Unmarked. The invention seems to us to be by Rosso. Probably 1542.

41 PAYSAGE DANS UN ENCADREMENT ORNEMENTAL (LANDSCAPE WITHIN AN ORNAMENTAL FRAME). H9. 225 × 382.
Monogram at bottom slightly to left. These ornaments in the style of Rosso seem to belong to a monumental decoration, but its origin is unknown. 1542–43.

42 PANNEAU D'ORNEMENTS AUTOUR D'UN CERCLE VIDE (PANEL OF ORNAMENTS AROUND AN EMPTY CIRCLE). H97 anonymous. 330 × 256.
Unmarked. Berliner's suggested attribution to Fantuzzi seems to us indisputable. 1542–43.

43 PAYSAGE DANS UN PANNEAU D'ORNEMENTS (LANDSCAPE WITHIN A PANEL OF ORNAMENTS). H126 anonymous. 231 × 395.
Unmarked. The attribution to Fantuzzi seems certain to us. 1542–43.

44 PAYSAGE DANS DES ORNEMENTS (LANDSCAPE WITHIN ORNAMENTS). H6. 323 (centre) × 508.
Monogram at bottom a little to the left. This seems to be a mural decoration, but we know neither its origin nor its author. 1542–43.

45 MONTANT D'ORNEMENT CARRÉ (UPRIGHT OF A SQUARE ORNAMENT). H11. 243 × 251.
Unmarked. The British Museum proof reproduced here bears a handwritten reference to Primaticcio, but the writing is not very old. Probably 1543.

46 PANNEAU D'ORNEMENT AVEC UN OVALE VIDE (ORNAMENTAL PANEL WITH AN EMPTY OVAL). H19. 268 × 325.
Unmarked. The Louvre has a drawing in reverse with small variations (Inv. 1,588); its author is unknown, but may be Fantuzzi himself. 1542–43.

47 PANNEAU D'ORNEMENT AVEC CERCLE VIDE (ORNAMENTAL PANEL WITH EMPTY CIRCLE). H20. 293 × 215.
Unmarked. 1542–43.

48 Variant of 47 with a landscape in the centre. H21. 252 × 143.
Unmarked. As Herbet observed, the attribution of

this repeat to Fantuzzi is not certain, but it seems to us possible. 1543?

49 PANNEAU D'ORNEMENT (ORNAMENTAL PANEL). H12. 242 × 316.
Unmarked. This seems to be a segment of a larger decorative composition whose author is unknown, but the print is complete. Probably 1543.

50 STATUE ANTIQUE DANS UN ENCADREMENT (ANTIQUE STATUE IN A FRAME). H56. 395 × 265.
Monogram at bottom right. Two states exist: in the second, the plate is shadowed with vertical hatching at top and bottom beyond the frame, whereas in the first these parts are white. The plate had previously been used and was badly erased. The dimensions and what one can see of the subject make us think that it is a piece of the 'Frieze of Sigismond' after Giulio Romano; but it is not one of the known plates. 1542–43.

51 PANNEAU D'ORNEMENT AVEC OVALE VIDE (OR-NAMENTAL PANEL WITH EMPTY OVAL). H8. 385 × 250.
Unmarked. What Bartsch and Herbet describe as a monogram in the small cartouche above the letter F is just a part of the design. Nevertheless the attribution is not doubtful. 1542–43.

52 CINQ VASES (FIVE VASES). H24. 175 × 327.
Unmarked. 1542–43.

53 CINQ VASES. H25. 173 × 325.

54a UNE AIGUIÈRE (A EWER). H23.

54b UNE GRANDE COUPE (A LARGE COVERED DISH). H23. Altogether 296 × 403?
Unmarked: the date 1543 is at the foot of the stand. These lovely vessels may have been designed by Rosso. The lobster-motif on the ewer is related to the reper-tory of Bernard Palissy. 54b is a first state, before the fretting of the plate that one sees in 54a; besides, in the second state, the child seen between the satyr's legs has his left shoulder crossed by mistake with a strong line. Dated 1543.

55 JUPITER ENVOYANT LES TROIS DÉESSES AU JUGEMENT DE PÂRIS (JUPITER SENDING THE THREE GODDESSES TO THE JUDGMENT OF PARIS). H18. 347 × 500.
Monogram and date at bottom towards the right. We part of the plate is corrected with the burin (Albertina). We believe it is a composition by Primaticcio of which all trace is lost. Dated 1543.

56 SILÈNE PORTÉ PAR DEUX BACCHANTS (SILENUS CARRIED BY TWO ATTENDANTS OF BACCHUS). Monogram and date at bottom towards the right. We agree with Kusenberg that the composition is by Giulio Romano and not Rosso. Dated 1543.

57 LE BANQUET DE SCIPION (SCIPIO'S BANQUET). H61. 395 × 570.
Monogram and date at bottom right. This composi-tion by Giulio Romano was part of the Triumphs of Scipio, a tapestry woven in Brussels, under Primatic-cio's supervision, for François I. An original drawing at Chantilly is probably the one used by the etcher; there is another less finished one in the Royal Collec-tion at Windsor. Dated 1543.

58 LA CONTINENCE DE SCIPION (SCIPIO'S CON-TINENCE). H57. Oval. 170 × 255.
Monogram and date at bottom left. Composition by Giulio Romano, also made into a print by Diana Scultori and painted in the Sala di Cesare, Palazzo de Tè. Dated 1543.

59 VÉNUS ET LES NYMPHES AU BAIN (VENUS AND NYMPHS BATHING). H78. Arched height 256 × 191.
At bottom right the inscription FR[ancescus] PA[rmigianus] INV[enit], the monogram and the date. Parmigianino's original drawing, of which Ugo da Carpi also made a chiaroscuro, is in the Uffizi, Florence. Dated 1543.

60 MONTANT D'ORNEMENT AVEC UN PETIT OVALE VIDE (ORNAMENT WITH A SMALL EMPTY OVAL). H7. 345 × 215.
Monogram at bottom centre. This very successful ornament is not exactly in the taste of either Rosso or Primaticcio; maybe it is an invention of Fantuzzi's. Probably 1543.

61 PAYSAGE DANS UN ENCADREMENT ORNEMEN-TAL (LANDSCAPE WITHIN AN ORNAMENTAL FRAME). H15. 277 × 266.
Unmarked. The ornament seems to be a mantelpiece, but it is probable that Fantuzzi replaced some com-position with figures by a landscape. Probably 1543.

62 JÉSUS LAVANT LES PIEDS DES DISCIPLES (JESUS WASHING THE DISCIPLES' FEET). H62. 330 × 470.
Unmarked. The attribution of the design to Giulio Romano seems to us very likely. Probably 1543.

63 CÉSAR FAISANT BRÛLER LES LETTRES DE POMPÉE (CAESAR BURNING POMPEY'S LETTERS). H65. Arched height 330 × 513.
Unmarked. The surprising appearance of this print may be explained by the unusual combination of dry-point and etching; the attribution to Fantuzzi seems

to us well-founded. The composition by Giulio Romano is painted in the Sala di Cesare, Palazzo del Tè. Probably 1543.

64 L'ÉTERNEL ASSIS SUR LE GLOBE (GOD SEATED ON THE GLOBE OF THE WORLD). H59 (L.D.). Arched top 228 × 450.
Unmarked. The attribution to Fantuzzi suggested in Lieure's notes is surely correct. As for the author of this surprising composition, the names of Rosso (Herbet) and Penni (Kusenberg) are not very satisfactory and perhaps one must search for him among the French. Probably 1543.

65 LA NATIVITÉ (THE NATIVITY). H8 anonymous. 276 × 220.
Bartsch did not detect the monogram on the right-hand upright of the trough. Herbet does not seem to have seen this piece. The composition strongly resembles the very original Nativities of Dumoûtier, and perhaps this is based on his design. Probably 1543.

66 PIETÀ. H28 anonymous. 324 × 236.
Unmarked. The quality of the line, the method of accentuating the contour, and the use of stipple seem to us to sanction the attribution to Fantuzzi. Rosso is surely the author of this admirable composition, of which no other version is known. Probably 1543.

67 HERCULE ET CACUS (HERCULES AND CACUS). H n.d. Bartsch 59 anonymous. 270 × 128.
Unmarked. Fantuzzi seems to us the only possible author of this beautiful print which Herbet failed to describe. Kusenberg cited Rosso as the author of the composition – rightly, we believe. The subject is described as Hercules and Antaeus by Bartsch. Probably 1543.

68 MARS ET VÉNUS AU BAIN (MARS AND VENUS BATHING). H54. Lunette. 215 × 445.
Monogram at right. Composition by Primaticcio, of which an original drawing is in the Louvre. It is not known where it was intended for. Probably 1543.

69 JASON LABOURANT LE CHAMP OU IL A SEMÉ LES DENTS DU DRAGON (JASON TILLING THE FIELD WHERE HE SOWED THE DRAGON'S TEETH). H50. 230 × 260.
Monogram at bottom left. The composition is certainly by Primaticcio and is a pendant to our No. 16 (L.D.). It is probably part of a decorative ensemble of which we have lost trace. 1543-44.

70 JEUNE HOMME ET JEUNE FEMME ASSIS SUR UN LIT (YOUNG MAN AND YOUNG WOMAN SITTING ON A BED). H48. Diameter 245.
Monogram at bottom right. The composition must be by Primaticcio and among his earliest work in France. Dimier refuses to acknowledge the subject as Achilles bidding farewell to the daughter of Lycomedes because he does not find the figure of Ulysses. We think he is perhaps the man in the middle who draws the young man by his arm. If this is the case, the composition would have been painted in the Chamber of Saint Louis. 1543-44.

71 JUPITER ET ANTIOPE (JUPITER AND ANTIOPE). H51. 170 × 263.
Monogram at bottom left. There are prints of this composition by Ferdinand and by Giorgio Ghisi. The latter confirms in his inscription that it is a decoration by Primaticcio at Fontainebleau. The Albertina has a drawing of it. Our No. 15 (L.D.) is a pendant to this composition, proven by the keystone which is repeated. It is not known where these decorations were painted. Probably 1544.

72 SATURNE ENDORMI (?) (SATURN ASLEEP). H44. Oval 242 × 359.
At bottom, the inscription 'Bologna Invento', the monogram and the date. This composition by Primaticcio, of which the Louvre has an original drawing, was painted on the vault in the vestibule of the Porte Dorée. Dated 1544.

73 UNE SYBILLE (A SYBIL). H53. 169 × 232.
Monogram at bottom left. This is surely a composition by Primaticcio. 1544-45.

74 SAINTE FAMILLE (THE HOLY FAMILY). H38. 332 × 270.
Monogram at left, towards the centre. It is generally agreed that this is a composition by Rosso; Panofsky sees in it a religious allegory rather than a simple Holy Family. There are two copies of it (Master I. ♀.V. and anonymous). 1544-45.

75 MÉLÉAGRE APPORTE À ATALANTE LA HURE DU SANGLIER (MELEAGER BRINGING THE BOAR'S HEAD TO ATLANTA). H55. Arched height 242 × 497.
Monogram at bottom towards the right. The author of this composition seems to us to be Rosso, whose style Fantuzzi has given a Primaticcian interpretation. It is not known where this lunette was painted. 1544-45.

76a CONCOURS D'APOLLON ET DE MARSYAS (CONTEST BETWEEN APOLLO AND MARSYAS). H77. 167 × 147.

76b SUPPLICE DE MARSYAS (THE FLAYING OF MARSYAS). H45. anonymous. 172 × 141.
Mariette describes a sheet in which three subjects were represented. The difference in height between 76a and 76b can be explained by the fact that the proofs

measured are trimmed. The attribution of 76b to Fantuzzi is in any case demanded by the style. We have not been able to find the third subject and, even less, an entire sheet. The invention is by Parmigianino. There is also a chiaroscuro of 76a. 1544-45.

77 JASON OU LA SURPRISE (JASON, OR THE SURPRISE). H79. 210 × 120.
Monogram at lower right. There exists a chiaroscuro, attributed to Niccolò Vicentino, of this composition by Parmigianino, of which the original drawing is in the Louvre. It is thought that the subject is Jason discovering the sea. Probably 1545.

78 GRAND CARTOUCHE OVALE VIDE (LARGE EMPTY OVAL CARTOUCHE). H17. 425 × 280.
Monogram at bottom right. 1544-45.

79 CARTOUCHE RECTANGULAIRE VIDE (EMPTY RECTANGULAR CARTOUCHE). H10. 293 × 418.
Monogram at bottom centre. There is a copy in reverse with a landscape in the cartouche (Herbet 116 anonymous). 1544-45.

80 GRAND ENCADREMENT ARCHITECTURAL (LARGE ARCHITECTURAL FRAME). H122 anonymous. 426 × 330.
Unmarked. Comparing this with the preceding two pieces, we feel the attribution to Fantuzzi is unquestionable. 1544-45.

81 LES FILLES DE MINÉE (THE DAUGHTERS OF MINYAS). H52. 250 × 307.
Inscription at the top of the loom: 'Bologa. InnVentor. Antonio Fantuzzi Fecit 1545'; and at the bottom: 'Mineia Proles' and 'ALCYTOE.CVM.SORORIBVS.IN.VESPERTILIONES'. It is not known what this delightful composition of Primaticcio's was intended for. A drawing in the Albertina appears to be a copy. Dated 1545.

82 UN CRYPTOPORTIQUE (A CRYPTO-PORCH). H22. 295 × 435.
The inscription on the tablets at the top can be read thus: 'ANTONIO FANTUZI DE BOLOGNA FECIT ANNO DOMINI M D 45'. This is not precisely the crypto-porch for the grotto of the Jardin des Pins (etched by Master L.D., our No. 60), but a rather more complicated invention, surmounted by an attic and leading into an interior courtyard. Primaticcio is probably the author of the design. Dated 1545.

83 LA CHUTE DE PHAÉTON (THE FALL OF PHAÉTON). H47. 256 × 382.
The inscription at bottom right is to be read as: 'Bologna inventor. Antonio Fantuzi Fecit 1545.' This is evidently a composition by Primaticcio for a ceiling, but it is not known where it was to be. There exists another anonymous engraving of it. Dated 1545.

84-111 STATUES ANTIQUES (ANTIQUE STATUES).
We have grouped at the end of Fantuzzi's œuvre his interpretations of antique statues. We believe that they were done between 1543 and 1545; in any case they show a variety of styles. It seemed to us that if we had grouped them at one period, 1543 for example, they would have interrupted the development of the œuvre, and it would have been unsuitable to disperse them arbitrarily. We cannot doubt that they deal with drawings from the antique brought back by Primaticcio and are not direct interpretations of the etcher. The nature of the drawing indicates this sufficiently, but there are also confirmations: the resemblance of style with the two statues etched by L.D. (our Nos 18 and 19); the existence of at least one original drawing by Primaticcio for *Hygieia* (No. 109 below) which belonged to Philippe de Chennevières and which we have unfortunately not been able to find (cf. L. Dimier, p. 469, No. 231; a sketch in his own copy at the Cabinet des Estampes of the Bibliothèque Nationale permits the identification). Two pieces are dated 1543. They may not be the earliest, but we do not think there were any much earlier. The rest are not dated. We have grouped them in order to follow, as well as possible, the etcher's development. Several plates bear Roman numerals, but since we have not been able to reconstitute the series, we have ignored these.

84 FEMME SUR LA POINTE DES PIEDS (WOMAN ON TIPTOES). H101. 277 × 141, sheet size.
Inscription at bottom: 'Roma. D. Latiano. Ivvenale. 1543 ANT. FAN.' The beginning of the inscription refers to Latino Giovenale who controlled the exportation of ancient marbles and from whom Primaticcio obtained ancient works. He must have owned the statue when Primaticcio drew it. (Cf. B. Jestaz, 'L'exportation des marbres de Rome de 1535 à 1571', *Mélanges d'A.et d'H. de l'Ecole française de Rome*. 1963, 415-466. Dated 1543.

85 CYBÈLE (CYBELE). H86. 233 × 152.
Inscription at bottom: 'Roma. D[the rest of the word illegible]. Dl. san Gallo 1543. ANT. F.' The meaning escapes us. Dated 1543.

86 STATUE DE FEMME PORTANT UN BOUCLIER (STATUE OF WOMAN CARRYING A SHIELD). H94. 210 × 105.
Monogram faintly visible at bottom left and the number II. Probably 1543.

87 FEMME DE PROFIL À GAUCHE (WOMAN WITH LEFT PROFILE). H92?. 208 × 97, subject.
Monogram at bottom left. Probably 1543.

88 FEMME DE PROFIL À GAUCHE (WOMAN WITH LEFT PROFILE). H96. 228 × 107, sheet.

Unmarked, at least on the trimmed impression of the Ecole des Beaux-Arts. Probably 1543.

89 FEMME DE PROFIL À DROITE (WOMAN WITH RIGHT PROFILE). H95. 212 × 92.
Unmarked. 1543–44.

90 STATUE DE FEMME DE PROFIL TOURNÉE À DROITE (STATUE OF WOMAN WITH PROFILE TURNED TOWARDS RIGHT). H n.d.
Monogram at bottom right. 1543–44.

91 MELPOMÈNE (MELPOMENE). H n.d.
Monogram at bottom left. Zava Boccazzi reproduced this, thinking it was Herbet 102 (our No. 104). 1543–44.

92 DEUX FEMMES (TWO WOMEN). H100. 190 × 110, subject.
Monogram at bottom centre and number I at left. 1543–44.

93 FEMME DEVANT UNE DRAPERIE (WOMAN IN FRONT OF A DRAPERY). H n.d. Bartsch 13. 227 × 133.
Monogram at left, and in the centre of the pedestal '.Roma.'. This is not No. 89 of Herbet, who refers to Bartsch 13 by error. 1543–44.

94 FEMME DE PROFIL À GAUCHE (WOMAN WITH LEFT PROFILE). H n.d. 213 × 100.
Unmarked, but the impression is cut. Probably 1544.

95 STATUE DE L'ABONDANCE (STATUE OF ABUN-DANCE). H97. 228 × 132.
Monogram at bottom left. Probably 1544.

96 FEMME TOURNÉE VERS LA DROITE, LE VISAGE DE PROFIL (WOMAN TURNED TOWARDS THE RIGHT, HER FACE IN PROFILE). H91. 220 × 81 subject.
Monogram at bottom left.

97 FEMME TOURNÉE À DROITE, LE VISAGE DE PRO-FIL À GAUCHE (WOMAN TURNED TO THE RIGHT, HER FACE IN LEFT PROFILE). H98. 250 × 100.
Monogram at bottom. 1544–45.

98 FEMME DE FACE, LA TÊTE UN PEU À GAUCHE (WOMAN FULL FACE, HER HEAD SLIGHTLY TO THE LEFT). H88. 267 × 88, subject.
Monogram at bottom left. 1544–45.

99 FEMME DE FACE (WOMAN FULL FACE). H n.d. 239 × 116.
Monogram at bottom left and numeral I.I.I.I. 1544–45.

100 MELPOMÈNE (MELPOMENE). H. n.d. 232 × 97.
Unmarked. Phyllis D. Massar ('Source of a Rare

Ecole de Fontainebleau Etching' in *Art Bulletin* XLVII, 1965) correctly attributed this sheet to Fantuzzi, and found the antique model for it in the sarcophagus of the Muses in the Mattei Collection in the Museo dei Termi, Rome. 1544–45.

101 EUTERPE. H85. 249 × 94.
Monogram at bottom left. The antique model found by P. Massar is the same sarcophagus as No. 100. 1544–45.

102 JEUNE FEMME DANSANT (YOUNG WOMAN DANCING). H93. 231 × 133.
Monogram at bottom right. 1544–45.

103 FEMME DE FACE, LA TÊTE UN PEU À GAUCHE (WOMAN FULL FACE, HER HEAD SLIGHTLY TO THE LEFT). H n.d. 257 × 145.
Monogram at bottom and numeral XII at left. Probably 1545.

104 MELPOMÈNE. H102. 221 × 87, subject.
Monogram at right on pedestal. Probably 1545.

105 MINERVE (MINERVA). H104. 246 × 115.
Unmarked in the first state. The second has a mono-gram at right on the pedestal. Herbet describes a third state in which the monogram is badly erased and replaced with the number 72. Probably 1545.

106 HYGIE (HYGIEIA). H105. 235 × 127.
Unmarked. Probably 1545.

107 FEMME LES JAMBES CROISÉES (WOMAN WITH CROSSED LEGS). H99. 220 × 87.
Unmarked, at least on the trimmed impression. Probably 1545.

108 FEMME DE FACE, LA TÊTE INCLINÉE À DROITE (WOMAN FULL FACE, HER HEAD INCLINED TOWARDS THE RIGHT). H89. 233 × 97, subject.
Monogram at right. This is not, as Herbet indicates, Bartsch's 13 (see our No. 93). Probably 1545.

109 HYGIE (HYGIEIA). H87. 233 × 89, subject.
Monogram at right. The original drawing by Prima-ticcio (now lost) belonged to Philippe de Chennevi-ères. Probably 1545.

110 FEMME ASSISE SUR UN FAUTEUIL (WOMAN SEATED IN AN ARMCHAIR). H90. 215 × 115.
Monogram at top left. Probably 1545.

111 EMPEREUR DANS UNE NICHE (EMPEROR IN A NICHE). H103. 240 × 101, the niche.
Monogram at bottom right. It is not certain that this is an antique statue. In any case, the design seems to us to be by Primaticcio. Probably 1545.

L. D.

As in the case of Fantuzzi, we have arranged the prints by L.D. in an approximate chronological order, believing that, even though extremely hypothetical, this would be more enlightening than by order of subject. But we have not tried to give approximate dates because there is a lack of assured guideposts.

We have excluded from the œuvre of L.D. certain attributions which seem to us mistaken. Aside from such pieces as will be found in this book under other artists, these are: the *Monogramme de Jésus* (H41), a piece without much character; *Cinq amours qui se jettent des pommes* (H54), a harsh and badly drawn etching; *Jeune femme debout tenant un rameau d'olivier* (H61) which, if it is by L.D., forms part of a group of late works (see Introduction); *La Dispute d'Apollon et de Marsyas* (H38), which is perhaps by Master I.♀.V.; and *Deux statues antiques* (H95), which Herbet knew only from the catalogue of the Robert-Dumesnil sale of 1862, which has not been found, and which may be nothing more than an impression of the print by Fantuzzi (F92).

I ENGRAVINGS

1 JEUNE FEMME QUI PLEURE (YOUNG WOMAN CRYING), Psyche. H84. 277 × 194.
Monogram at bottom right. This is the central figure in the story of the ants dividing the grain in the Psyche fable, a composition by Giulio Romano painted in the Sala di Psiche, Palazzi del Tè, Mantua. We believe this to be the first known print by L.D.; 1540 at the latest.

2 L'AIGLE DE JUPITER APPORTÉ À PSYCHÉ DE L'EAU DU STYX (JUPITER'S EAGLE BRINGING THE WATER OF THE STYX TO PSYCHE). H82. 205 × 395.
Monogram at bottom right, and the inscription at left: 'IVLIVS INVENTOR'. This composition by Giulio Romano is painted in the Sala di Psiche, Palazzo del Tè.

3 JEUNE FEMME HABILLÉE À L'ANTIQUE (YOUNG WOMAN IN ANTIQUE DRESS). H87. 165 × 115.
Two monograms towards the top at left. The upper one has not been satisfactorily interpreted. We believe that IVR must be read as Iulius Romanus (compared with the inscription on L.D.2). The author of this composition must thus be Giulio Romano rather than Parmigianino, as Herbet thought. There are two other engraved versions known (anonymous Italian and A. Quesnel). Dated 1540.

4 LA DANSE (THE DANCE). H51. 330 × 465.
Monogram at centre bottom. The composition is probably by Giulio Romano and is painted in the Loggia della Grotta, Palazzo del Tè. The subject is the Dance and not Cupid aiming an arrow at Apollo's heart. An original preparatory drawing is in the Albertina.

5 L'AMOUR LES YEUX BANDÉS (CUPID WITH BANDAGED EYES). H49. 194 × 350.
Monogram at bottom towards left. The author of

the composition could be Rosso as well as Primaticcio, whose style is generally not so nervous and angular.

6 JUPITER PRESSANT LES NUÉES (JUPITER PRESSING THE STORMCLOUDS). H11. Arched top 240 × 443.
Monogram at bottom below Jupiter. The composition is surely by Primaticcio, but we do not know where this lunette was situated.

7 LE JARDIN DE VERTUMNE (THE GARDEN OF VERTUMNUS). H16. 334 × 335.
Below the statue of Priapus: 'A fontenebleau'. The monogram appears only in the second state at bottom left on a mound. The copies of the first state are often counterproofs. Composition by Primaticcio painted in the Pavilion of Pomona (see F38).

8 DANAË. H4. Oval 215 × 290.
Monogram at right. Composition by Primaticcio painted in the Galerie François I. Original drawing at the Musée Condé, Chantilly.

9 HERCULE COUCHÉ AUPRÈS D'OMPHALE (HERCULES IN BED WITH OMPHALE). H2. 221 × 410.
Monogram at bottom right. Composition by Primaticcio painted in the portico of the Porte Dorée. Original drawing in the collection of the Duke of Devonshire, Chatsworth.

II ETCHINGS

10 HERCULE SE LAISSANT HABILLER EN FEMME (HERCULES BEING DRESSED AS A WOMAN). H3. 281 × 434.
Monogram at bottom right. Composition by Primaticcio painted in the portico of the Porte Dorée; the original drawing in the Albertina. This was also etched by Fantuzzi (F17).

11 JUPITER ET SÉMÉLÉ (JUPITER AND SEMELE). H5. Oval 210 × 291.
Monogram on the foot of the bed towards the left. This composition by Primaticcio was painted in the small room which led to the Galerie François I and which was destroyed when the building was enlarged on that side of the gallery. The oval form makes it certain that it was this composition, rather than the other version (LD68), which was painted there.

12 CONCERT DE NYMPHES DANS UN PAYSAGE (CONCERT OF NYMPHS IN A LANDSCAPE). H47. 194 × 268.
Monogram towards bottom left. The composition is surely by Primaticcio.

13 DIANE AU REPOS (DIANA RESTING). H34. 152 (5 in the margin) × 283.
Monogram at bottom right, and in the centre of the margin: 'A. fonteñnbleau'. The composition is indisputably by Primaticcio and the inscription leads one to believe that it was painted in the Château of Fontainebleau, but it is not known where.

14 ANGE SONNANT DE LA TROMPE (ANGEL SOUNDING THE TRUMPET). H55. 250 × 152.
Unmarked. The attribution to L.D. seems to us indisputable. A drawing in the Louvre may be an original by Primaticcio retouched by Rubens.

15 NYMPHE MUTILANT UN SATYRE (NYMPH MUTILATING A SATYR). H7. 160 × 152.
Monogram at bottom towards left. Composition by Primaticcio. There is an anonymous etching copied in reverse from L.D. Original drawing in the Albertina. For a pendant, see F71.

16 JASON TUANT LE DRAGON (JASON SLAYING THE DRAGON). H48. 258 × 311.
Monogram at bottom centre. Composition by Primaticcio; see F69.

17 L'APOLLON DU BELVÉDÈRE (THE BELVEDERE APOLLO). H91. 286 × 161.
Monogram engraved on the base of the statue; the one at right is that of the publisher Visscher. Proofs without this mark probably exist. The printmaker must have reproduced a drawing by Primaticcio after the antique.

18 STATUE DE FEMME TOURNÉE VERS LA GAUCHE (STATUE OF A WOMAN TURNED TOWARDS THE LEFT). H94. 214 × 104.
Monogram at bottom towards left. Etching of a drawing by Primaticcio from the antique.

19 STATUE DE FEMME DE PROFIL À DROITE (STATUE OF A WOMAN WITH RIGHT PROFILE). H93. 221 × 93.

Monogram at bottom right. Etching of a drawing by Primaticcio from the antique.

20 CIRCÉ DONNANT UN BREUVAGE AUX COMPAGNONS D'ULYSSE (CIRCE GIVING A DRINK TO ULYSSES' COMPANIONS). H88. Diameter 224.
Monogram at bottom left. In a second state the plate has been reduced to the dimensions 175 × 223, in such a way that the top and bottom of the circle are truncated. Composition by Parmigianino, also etched by Fantuzzi (F18).

21 ÉROS ÉT ANTEROS (EROS AND ANTEROS). H53. 150 × 255.
Monogram at bottom left (not at right, as Herbet says). There is a copy by Ferdinand. The drawing is no doubt by Primaticcio.

22 MERCURE ENSEIGNANT LES ARTS (MERCURY TEACHING THE ARTS). H n.d. 178 × 298.
Monogram at bottom centre. Composition by Giulio Romano; the group at left with another figure in place of the bellows is executed in stucco on the ceiling of the Sala degli Stucchi, Palazzo del Tè.

23 RÉBECCA ET ELIÉZER (REBECCA AND ELIEZER). H35. Arched top 295 × 270.
Monogram at bottom right, and at centre: 'A Fontennebleau'. The composition, which is certainly by Primaticcio, was probably painted in the Château, but we do not know where. The original drawing is in the Louvre.

24 CLÉOPÂTRE PIQUÉE PAR UN ASPIC (CLEOPATRA BITTEN BY AN ASP). H43. 288 × 161.
Monogram in centre towards bottom. One can distinguish a second state by a strong stroke made by mistake on the right leg. Copy of a print by Agostino Veneziano after Baccio Bandinelli.

25–36 LES MUSES ET LES TROIS GRANDES DÉESSES (THE MUSES AND THE THREE GREAT GODDESSES).
These dozen figures were etched after Primaticcio, whose original drawings are in the Louvre, except for *Euterpe* (in the Musée Bonnat, Bayonne) and *Erato* (which is not known). Dimier has shown that these were most probably decorations for the lower gallery of the Château. There are engraved copies with the names in Greek characters. The etchings bear at the bottom 'Bologna/L.D.' and *Euterpe* has, in addition, the indication 'A fonteñnbleau'.

25 JUNO. H19. 223 × 173.

26 VENUS. H20. 232 × 171.

27 ATHENA. H21. 208 × 160.

28 CALLIOPE. H22. 213 × 162.

29 TERPSICHORE. H23. 225 × 176.

30 ERATO. H24. 223 × 174.

31 POLYHYMNIA. H25. 220 × 174.

32 URANIA. H26. 231 × 174.
There is an anonymous copy (Bartsch 56 of the Fontainebleau anonymous).

33 CLIO. H27. 220 × 173.

34 EUTERPE. H28. 233 × 165.

35 THALIA. H29. 217 × 173.

36 MELPOMÈNE. H30. 213 × 158.

37 NYMPHE REGARDANT UN HÉRON S'ENVOLER (NYMPH WATCHING A HERON FLYING AWAY). H33. 145 × 258.
Unmarked. The lack of regularity in the hatching and the hesitancy of the line makes us seriously doubt the attribution to L.D. But certain resemblances of style keep us from definitively rejecting the piece from the œuvre. The composition is by Primaticcio and an original drawing is in the Hermitage, Leningrad. Another drawing at Besançon may be a preparation by the etcher.

38 CHIENS ATTAQUANT UN CERF (DOGS ATTACKING A STAG). H38. 242 × 348.
Monogram at bottom left under the indication 'Bologna'. In a second state, there are oxydation spots in the sky. The composition is by Primaticcio and we think that it may concern Acteon devoured by his dogs, as Dimier suggested.

39 L'EMPEREUR MARC ANTOINE OFFRANT UN SACRIFICE (EMPEROR MARK ANTONY OFFERING A SACRIFICE). H57. 270 × 485.
The monogram is at the bottom of the altar; at bottom left and right are the numbers 74 and 75, but their significance escapes us. In a second state an inscription has been added which begins 'His et talibus . . .', and the plate, which is reduced in size, bears the indication 'Ant. Lafreri formis Romae' and the date MDLXV. It was published again in a third state with the mark, 'Petri de Nobilibus'. The plate probably reproduces a drawing by Primaticcio after Antonine's Column.

40 ENFANT NU TENANT UN AVIRON (NAKED CHILD WITH OAR). H227. 124 × 68.
Unmarked. The attribution to L.D. strikes us as very probable. After Primaticcio.

41 ENFANT NU TENANT UN AVIRON (NAKED CHILD WITH OAR. H228. 124 × 68.
Monogram F.P. at bottom left, which seems to signify Francesco Primaticcio. If the monogram is indeed in the plate, it is surprising since L.D. generally indicates 'Bologna', but the attribution to the etcher seems very probable even though L.D.'s monogram does not appear.

42 *Detail*, A KING KNEELING BEFORE AN ALTAR.
Detail of following.

42 UN ROI AGENOUILLÉ DEVANT UN AUTEL (A KING KNEELING BEFORE AN ALTAR). H n.d. 110 × 514.
Monogram at bottom centre. The composition, which is very Venetian in style, is completely surprising at Fontainebleau. The Primaticcian aspect of the figures probably comes from the etcher's interpretation. Should we see here a trace of Paris Bordone's passing through Fontainebleau? This exceptional piece leaves us perplexed, but there is no reason to doubt that it is by Master L.D.

43 L'ENLÈVEMENT D'EUROPE (THE RAPE OF EUROPA). H18. 234 × 218.
Monogram at bottom right and the indication 'Bologna'. The original drawing of the composition by Primaticcio is in the Louvre, but it is not known where it was intended for.

44-45 BELLONE ASSISE SUR SES TROPHÉES (BELLONA SEATED ON HER TROPHIES). H31. 150 × 206.
MARS ASSIS SUR DES TROPHÉES (MARS SEATED ON TROPHIES). H32. 153 × 203.
Monogram at bottom and indication 'Bologna' on each piece. These compositions by Primaticcio were probably painted in the Château but it is not known where. The original drawing of Bellona is in the Louvre. The impressions reproduced here are printed on the same sheet.

46 HERCULE COMBATTANT DE DESSUS LE VAISSEAU DES ARGONAUTES (HERCULES FIGHTING FROM THE ARGONAUTS' SHIP). H1. 233 × 343.
Monogram at bottom towards the centre. Somewhat higher, the indication 'BoLoGnA InVeNtor'. Composition by Primaticcio painted in the vestibule of the Porte Dorée; the original drawing in the Albertina. There is an engraved copy by Goltzius.

47 ACHILLE RETIRANT DU COMBAT LE CORPS DE PATROCLE (ACHILLES REMOVING PATROCLUS' BODY FROM THE BATTLE). H81. 353 × 585.
Monogram at bottom somewhat to right. This composition by Giulio Romano, of which there is another print by Diana Scultori, is painted in the Sala di Troia

in the Ducal Palace in Mantua. It may be that this etching by L.D. is a little later than the place where we have put it would indicate.

48 PYGMALION SCULPTANT GALATÉE (PYGMALION MAKING THE STATUE OF GALATEA). H52. 234 × 127.
Monogram on the pedestal of the statue. This print is doubtless after Primaticcio.

49 JUPITER ET ANTIOPE (JUPITER AND ANTIOPE). H10. 166 × 257.
Monogram at centre towards the bottom. The composition is most probably by Primaticcio, but it is not the one Fantuzzi etched, as Herbet indicates in his 'Additions'.

50-52 Compositions by Primaticcio painted in the chamber of Mme d'Etampes.

50 ALEXANDRE DOMPTANT BUCÉPHALE (ALEXANDER MASTERING BUCEPHALUS). H12. Oval 349 × 222.
Monogram at bottom and the indication 'Bol.'. In a second state one can read, 'F.L.D. Ciartes excu.'.

51 APELLE PEIGNANT ALEXANDRE ET CAMPASPE (APELLES PAINTING ALEXANDER AND CAMPASPE). H13. Oval 341 × 240.
Monogram on an overturned vase with the indication 'Bologna'.

52 TIMOCLÉE DEVANT ALEXANDRE (TIMOCLEIA BEFORE ALEXANDER). H37. Oval 318 × 210.
Monogram at bottom with the indication 'Bologna'.

53-56 LES APÔTRES CONTEMPLANT LE CHRIST ET LA VIERGE DANS DES GLOIRES D'ANGES (THE APOSTLES LOOKING AT CHRIST AND THE VIRGIN IN A GLORY OF ANGELS). H77-88.
The monogram on the two top parts towards the centre of each and in the margin of the bottom left piece towards the right, followed by the inscription 'Lion daven' astride the two bottom pieces; the date 1546 at the far right. This is a variation of the *Assumption*, a composition by Giulio Romano painted in the apse of Verona Cathedral; Christ has been added to the right of the Virgin. This variant seems to us an adaptation rather than an idea of Giulio Romano himself. Dated 1546.

53 Top left plate. 396 × 533.

54 Top right plate. 402 × 545.

55 Bottom left plate. 380 × 560.

56 Bottom right plate. 383 × 547.

57 SACRÉE CONVERSATION ('SACRED CONVERSATION'). H85. 242 × 183.
Monogram at bottom. The composition is by Parmigianino. There exists a free copy published by Jean Chartier of Orléans in 1557 (Robert-Dumesnil 1).

58 JUPITER. H90. 277 × 147.
Monogram at bottom towards the right. Herbet believed this print was after an antique statue, but the model for it is unknown. It is not impossible that it bears some relation to the statue of Jupiter made by Benvenuto Cellini at Fontainebleau.

59 HOMMES RASSEMBLÉS AUTOUR D'UN CHAMEAU (MEN GATHERED AROUND A CAMEL). H15. 320 × 435.
Monogram below the inscription, 'Bol. inventeur à Fontainebleau'. If this is meant to be an episode in the story of Joseph, it does not seem possible to us to see in it Joseph sold by his brothers, as Mariette proposed. Could it be the searching of Joseph's brothers' baggage? Thus it could be the picture in the Cabinet du Roi mentioned by Father Dan, 'une histoire représentant Joseph comme ses frères le sont venus visiter en Egypte' ('a story representing Joseph as his brothers came to visit him in Egypt'). There is another print in reverse of this composition by an anonymous artist (Herbet 67).

60 CRYPTOPORTIQUE DE LA GROTTE DU JARDIN DES PINS (CRYPTO-PORCH OF THE GROTTO OF THE JARDIN DES PINS). H17. 531 × 245, plate size.
Monogram on the keystone in the centre. The print probably reproduces a drawing by Primaticcio, a project very close to what one sees constructed at Fontainebleau.

61 UN SACRIFICE (A SACRIFICE). H50. 220 × 450.
Monogram at bottom left. The print evidently reproduces a drawing by Primaticcio, inspired perhaps by some antique model.

62 DEUX PRISONNIERS CONDUITS PAR DEUX SOLDATS ROMAINS (TWO PRISONERS BEING LED BY TWO ROMAN SOLDIERS). H56. 231 × 173.
Unmarked. The attribution seems to us very probable. The print certainly reproduces a drawing by Primaticcio, perhaps after the antique.

63 JÉSUS GUÉRISSANT DIX LÉPREUX (JESUS HEALING TEN LEPERS). H86. 285 × 403.
Unmarked. The attribution seems to us indisputable. The composition is by Parmigianino. There exists a chiaroscuro of it and another print by Meldolla, called Schiavone.

64 FEMME NUE DEBOUT (STANDING NUDE WOMAN). H45. 277 × 143.
Monogram on the chair at right. On the lower bar is the mark of the publisher Visscher, which does not appear in the first state. The invention must be by Primaticcio. It may be Venus, but nothing would indicate this except her beauty.

65 DEUX FEMMES NUES AVEC L'AMOUR (TWO NUDE WOMEN WITH CUPID). H44. 219 × 116.
The monogram of the engraver is at the bottom right, followed by another one whose meaning escapes us. The composition seems quite certainly to be by Primaticcio, but the subject remains obscure.

66 DEUX VIEILLARDS COUVERTS DE MANTEAUX (TWO OLD PERSONS WITH CLOAKS). H36. 248 × 302.
Monogram at bottom right with indication 'Bologna'. Perhaps the subjects are Philemon and Baucis. Dimier refers to a drawing at Dresden; McAllister Johnson has discovered another at Berlin (*Art Quarterly*, XXIX (1966), p. 255 and fig. 8).

67 VÉNUS DANS LA FORGE DE VULCAIN (VENUS AT VULCAN'S FORGE). H14. 322 × 444.
Monogram at bottom left. The composition is most probably by Luca Penni.

68 JUPITER ET SÉMÉLÉ (JUPITER AND SEMELE). H6. 210 × 291.
Monogram and 'Bologna' at bottom left. This composition by Primaticcio is not the one painted in the little room leading to the Galerie François I (see LD11).

69 CHAPITEAU D'ORDRE COMPOSITE (CAPITAL OF COMPOSITE ORDER). H n.d.? 288 × 338.
Unmarked. A second state bears an inscription which begins 'Ingentis Columnae . . .' followed by the name of the publisher Salamanca and the date 1560. The attribution of this superb etching to L.D. seems probable to us; it would have been executed after a drawing brought from Rome by Primaticcio.

70 LA MORT D'ADONIS (THE DEATH OF ADONIS). H61. 277 × 390.
Monogram at bottom left. The composition is probably by Penni.

71 TARQUIN ET LUCRÈCE (TARQUIN AND LUCRETIA). H74. 269 × 214. Monogram D.L. at bottom left. The attribution can hardly be doubted. Penni may be the author of the composition, as Herbet believed.

72 VÉNUS DÉCOUVRANT MARS ENDORMI (VENUS FINDING MARS ASLEEP). H12 of the work of I. ♀.V. 296 × 273.

Unmarked. Lieure believed this piece was etched by Mignon, but the style as well as the existence of several copies with counterproofs of prints by L.D. on the back make us attribute this sheet to the master without hesitation. The invention is perhaps by Penni.

73 LA MADELEINE TRANSPORTÉE AU CIEL (MARY MAGDALEN CARRIED TO HEAVEN). H76. 328 × 268.
Monogram at bottom. According to Mariette, the composition is by Giulio Romano, but Primaticcio seems to us possible too. There is an anonymous counterpart copy (Herbet 31).

74 MARS ET VÉNUS SERVIS À TABLE PAR L'AMOUR (MARS AND VENUS BEING SERVED AT TABLE BY CUPID). H73. 288 × 430.
Monogram at bottom right. The attribution of the composition to Penni is satisfactory.

75 CAMILLE ARRIVANT AU MOMENT OU LES RO-MAINS SE RACHÈTENT DU PILLAGE (CAMILLUS ARRIVING AT THE MOMENT WHEN THE ROMANS ATONE FOR THEIR PILLAGE). H42. 283 × 390.
Monogram at bottom left. The composition seems to us to be by Penni rather than Primaticcio. Dimier also rejected the latter attribution.

76 JUPITER ENTOURÉ DES AUTRES DIVINITÉS POR-TANT DES BRANCHES D'ARBRES (JUPITER SUR-ROUNDED BY OTHER GODS CARRYING BRANCHES). H46. 400 × 280.
Monogram on the cartouche which also has a quotation from Pliny and the date. We agree with Dimier in rejecting this composition from the œuvre of Primaticcio; perhaps it is by Penni. Dated 1547.

77-79 TROIS PIÈCES CONCERNANT LA PÊCHE ET LA CHASSE (THREE PRINTS ABOUT FISHING AND HUNTING).
Each piece is in an oval inscribed in a rectangle. Each plate bears the monogram and the date 1547 at bottom. There is a second state of No. 78, in which the plate has been reduced to the oval. These compositions are generally attributed to Luca Penni, but it seems to us that the figures, the continuity of space in depth, the method of linking the groups, are characteristic of Primaticcio. We believe that the invention of these admirable works must be attribu-ted to him. Dated 1547.

77 ADONIS POURSUIVANT LE SANGLIER DE CALY-DON (ADONIS PURSUING CALYDON'S BOAR). H62. 312 × 395.

78 DIANE ET SES NYMPHES POURSUIVANT UN CERF (DIANA AND HER NYMPHS PURSUING A STAG). H63. 320 × 390.

79 SCÈNE DE PÊCHE (FISHING SCENE). H64. 379 × 312.

80 COMBAT DES AMAZONES (BATTLE OF AMAZONS).
H92. 182 × 415.
Monogram at bottom centre and the date a bit to the
right. It is not known where the composition comes
from. Dated 1547.

81 FEMME PORTÉE VERS UN SATYRE LIBIDINEUX
(WOMAN BEING CARRIED TO A LIBIDINOUS
SATYR). H8. 236 × 424.
Monogram and date at bottom centre. The original
drawing by Primaticcio, with the satyr cut off,
belongs to Robert Lehman, New York. Dated 1547.

82 SATYRE PORTÉ VERS UNE FEMME (SATYR BEING
CARRIED TO A WOMAN). H9. 226 × 400.
Monogram at left. The original drawing by Prima-
ticcio, with the woman cut off, is in the Hermitage,
Leningrad. Dated 1547 by the pendant.

83 DANSE DE FAUNES ET DE BACCHANTES (DANCE
OF FAUNS AND BACCHANTES). H89. 174 × 491.
Monogram at bottom towards the right (not at top,
as Herbet says). Herbet also says that the print is
arched, but we do not think so. Etched after a print
by Agostino Veneziano.

84 LE CHRIST AUX LIMBES (CHRIST IN LIMBO). H40.
356 × 284.
Monogram at bottom centre. Dimier included this
sheet in his catalogue of prints after Primaticcio, but
it seems to us much more like an invention of Luca
Penni, because of the types and the composition on a
plane, close to what one sees in the *Capital Sins* below.

85-92 LES PÉCHÉS CAPITAUX (THE CAPITAL SINS).
Suite of eight prints from inventions by Luca Penni,
as indicated in the inscription on the frontispiece.
Besides, the artist owned the copperplates of the prints
when he died. Master L.D. etched the whole series,
with the exception of *Paresse* (No. 92) which is by
another anonymous artist; this same artist also finished
L'Impudicité (No. 91), and retouched the other plates
which thus exist in two very distinct states. In the
first, the plate is light and executed in pure etching; in
the second, the plate is retouched with the burin and
becomes darker and more contrasted. Only the two
last plates remain unchanged. We believe it is probable that this series was executed in 1547 or shortly
thereafter.

85 LA JUSTICE (JUSTICE). Frontispiece. H65. 310 × 420.
Monogram at left on a vat. At the bottom inscribed:
'SVB PENNIS EIVS ERO L. PENNIS R.

85*bis* Frontispiece: second state. The plate is entirely
retouched; the monogram is no longer legible.

86 L'ORGUEIL (PRIDE). H66. 300 × 460.

87 L'AVARICE (AVARICE). H67. 300 × 460.

88 L'ENVIE (ENVY). H69. 300 × 460.

89 LE GOURMANDISE (GREED). H70. 300 × 460.

90 LA COLÈRE (ANGER). H71. 300 × 460.

91 L'IMPUDICITÉ (LUST). H68. 300 × 460.
This plate was finished by an anonymous printmaker.

92 LA PARESSE (SLOTH). H72. 300 × 460.
This plate is not by L.D., but the work of an artist
who remains anonymous. One might think of Luca
Penni himself.

93 UNE FEMME MONTRANT DES TAUREAUX À UN
HOMME (A WOMAN SHOWING BULLS TO A MAN).
H58. 168 × 217.
Monogram at bottom centre, and inscription in the
margin: 'Cum privilegio Regis'. Dimier quite rightly
did not retain this composition in the œuvre of
Primaticcio; we are perplexed to assign it an author.
This plate is part of a group of late works by L.D., of
which we give only a few examples.

94 SUR LA MALÉDICTION DE CÉRÈS, UN DES BŒUFS
QUI TRAINENT UNE CHARRUE TOMBE SUR LES
GENOUX (UNDER CERES' CURSE, ONE OF THE
OXEN DRAWING A PLOUGH FALLS TO ITS KNEES).
H163. 132 with margin × 225.
Unmarked; but the attribution is confirmed by the
rest of the series. This is plate 7 of a series of twelve
sheets on the Love of Pluto and Proserpine, from the
invention of Léonard Thiry. After 1547.

95 L'ENLÈVEMENT D'AMYMONE (THE ABDUCTION
OF AMYMONE). H184. 165 × 235.
Monogram at bottom right. This plate is part of a
whole group of landscapes, generally with figures, of
which L.D. etched the most, but of which several
pieces are by a different hand. M. Philippe de Montebello has been kind enough to inform me of the exact
correspondence of the plate described by Herbet
under his No. 218 with a drawing in the British
Museum. This drawing is in the same style as those
attributed by Otto Benesch to Jean Cousin the
Younger. In our opinion, it is not impossible that
the anonymous printmaker who collaborated with
L.D. and who is the author of Herbet's No. 218 may
be the designer himself. (See our p. 22, n. 1, Introduction.)

96-98 Plates from *Les quatre premiers livres des Navigations
et pérégrinations orientales de N. de Nicolay . . .*, published at Lyons by Guillaume Rouille in 1567 or 1568.

The 61 plates in this book are by L.D. who marked nearly all of them. The licence is dated 1555, and one of the plates (our 98) bears the date 1556. It is not known what delayed publication.

96 FEMME DE L'ISLE DE CHIO (WOMAN FROM THE ISLAND OF CHIOS). H100. 270 × 175. Monogram towards the left.

97 VILLAGEOIS GREC (GREEK VILLAGER). H127. 270 × 175.
Monogram at right.

98 CADILESQUER (TURKISH JUDGE). H128. 270 × 175. Monogram towards the bottom at right and date at centre. Dated 1556.

JEAN MIGNON

As with the preceding printmakers, we have arranged Mignon's work in approximate chronological order, while keeping the different series intact, such as the Terminals and the story of Troy. There are not sufficient guides for dating a large part of the work, but we are convinced that Mignon's prints were executed in a comparatively short span of time, probably beginning in 1543 and ending perhaps not much later than 1545.

We have rejected three pieces catalogued by Herbet under Mignon's name: *La Flagellation* (H5) which seems to us to be by the printmaker who marked one etching with the monogram GR; *Les Disciples déposant le corps de Jésus* (H7), which is from a drawing by Penni but etched by a hand which seems to us cruder and different from Mignon's; and *Mars et Vénus sur un lit magnifique* (H18), which may also be by Master GR.

1 SAINTE FAMILLE (HOLY FAMILY). H16 anonymous. 350 × 253.
Unmarked; the date at top in a little cartouche. The drawing, the treatment of the draperies and the conception of space appear to us very close to JM6 and also the signed piece JM7. The author of this remarkable composition is unknown. The name of Giulio Romano suggested by Herbet does not seem convincing. There are resemblances to certain figures by Luca Penni, but also to the pieces which follow and which do not seem to be his designs. Dated 1543.

2 L'ADORATION DES BERGERS (ADORATION OF THE SHEPHERDS). H10 anonymous. 210 × 182.
Unmarked; date at bottom left. This print seems to us to be clearly by the same hand as the preceding piece, and the attribution is made for that reason. The design could also be by the same master; in that case, this piece would make a link between the preceding one and the three that follow. Dated 1544.

3 SAINTE FAMILLE (HOLY FAMILY). H23 anonymous. 233 × 162.
Unmarked and undated. The drawing, the morphology of the vegetation, and the taste of the landscape seem to attach this piece to JM5 and JM6, and therefore to the œuvre of Mignon. The characters are very similar to those of the two following compositions. A print, unfortunately lost but reproduced in the *Atlas Jean Cousin* by Firmin Didot, is in very much the same style and bears the indication 'I.C.inv.'. It is not impossible that we must see in this the invention of Jean Cousin. 1543-44.

4 SAINTE FAMILLE (HOLY FAMILY). H26. 250 × 315.
Unmarked. It was Renouvier who first attributed to Mignon this beautiful plate carefully finished off with the burin. It seems to us harmonious with the preceding pieces, particularly JM2. It is all the more interesting to note that it was its relations with other works by Mignon, such as the Trojan series, which suggested to Renouvier the possibility of this attribution. For the author of the composition, see JM3. 1544?

5 LA SAINTE FAMILLE AUX OISEAUX (HOLY FAMILY WITH BIRDS). H17 anonymous. 306 × 222.
Unmarked. Clearly by the same hand as the following piece. The very distinctive vegetation, the treatment of the drapery, the method of bringing everything to the surface, seem to us to reveal Jean Mignon (see particularly JM29 and JM32). For the author of the composition (who could not be Rosso, as Herbet suggests) see JM3. Probably 1544.

6 LA CHARITÉ (CHARITY). H19 of I. ♀.V. 270 × 189.
Unmarked; date at bottom. The style is not at all like Master I. ♀.V.'s, but Herbet had not seen the print. The composition is that of the well-known painting by Andrea del Sarto in the Louvre, in reverse, but the landscape is entirely changed: this was a habit of Mignon's. Dated 1544.

7 ENCADREMENT ORNEMENTAL (ORNAMENTAL FRAME). H25. 244 × 236. Signed and dated at bottom left: 'Ɩo MIGŌn. 1544.'. This ornamental composition is adapted from one by Primaticcio intended for the

chamber of Madame d'Etampes and which can still be seen. A drawing in the Louvre (RF 560) seems to have served as the model for the print. The style recalls that of a drawing in the Louvre (Inv. 1396) that is attributed to Penni.

8 PRIAM PAYANT LA RANÇON D'HECTOR (PRIAM PAYING RANSOM FOR HECTOR). H24. 166×220 oval.
Signed at bottom left. It is not impossible that Primaticcio was the author of this very well constructed composition. We are not certain that the subject we suggest is correct, but the figure carrying the balance is certainly a bearded old man and not a woman, as it has been described since Bartsch. The young man standing behind Priam could, with some licence, be Hermes even though Homer does not have him enter Achilles' tent.

9-28 SÉRIE DE VINGT TERMES (SERIES OF TWENTY TERMINALS)
This suite exists in two different states. In the first, the plates bear no mark or number. The last six, which have never been marked, have been slightly reduced. In the second state, the first fourteen plates are numbered, the first bearing in addition the indication: 'F.L.D. Ciartes excu'. This was therefore a printing of the seventeenth century. Like Lieure, we believe that this series was executed by Jean Mignon. The motifs are borrowed from various sources, and the series is probably a compilation made by Mignon. We cannot say why Herbet catalogued them as anonymous engravings, for the sheets are almost entirely etched. 215 to 235×125 to 145.

9 FEMME PORTANT UN PANIER SUR LA TÊTE (WOMAN CARRYING A BASKET ON HER HEAD). H1 anonymous engravings.

10 SATYRE PENCHÉ À DROITE (SATYR BENDING TOWARDS THE RIGHT). H2 anonymous engravings.

11 FEMME TENANT UN INSTRUMENT DE MUSIQUE (WOMAN WITH MUSICAL INSTRUMENT). H3 anonymous engravings.

12 HOMME DANS UNE NICHE (MAN IN A NICHE). H4 anonymous engravings.

13 GÉNIE CORNU (HORNED GENIUS). H5 anonymous engravings.

14 TÊTE DE FEMME SUR UN PIÉDESTAL (WOMAN'S HEAD ON A PEDESTAL). H6 anonymous engravings.

15 HERCULE ARMÉ DE LA MASSUE (HERCULES WITH HIS CLUB). H7 anonymous engravings.

16 SPHINGE PORTANT UN CROISSANT SUR LES CHEVEUX (SPHINX WEARING A CRESCENT ON HER HAIR). H8 anonymous engravings.

17 TÊTE BARBUE SUR UN PIÉDESTAL (BEARDED HEAD ON A PEDESTAL). H9 anonymous engravings.

18 LA DIANE D'ÉPHÈSE (DIANA OF EPHESUS). H10 anonymous engravings.

19 FEMME DE PROFIL À GAUCHE (WOMAN WITH LEFT PROFILE). H11 anonymous engravings.

20 SATYRE À JAMBES TORDUES (SATYR WITH TWISTED LEGS). H12 anonymous engravings.

21 PAN. H13 anonymous engravings.

22 VIEILLARD SE CHAUFFANT LES MAINS (OLD MAN WARMING HIS HANDS). H14 anonymous engravings.

23 FEMME TENANT UN VASE (WOMAN CARRYING A VASE). H15 anonymous engravings.

24 BACCHUS. H16 anonymous engravings.

25 SATYRE DANS UNE NICHE (SATYR IN A NICHE). H17 anonymous engravings.

26 HOMME BARBU, LES BRAS CROISÉS (BEARDED MAN WITH CROSSED ARMS). H18 anonymous engravings.

27 TÊTE ENTRE DEUX AIGLES (HEAD BETWEEN TWO EAGLES). H19 anonymous engravings.

28 CARIATIDE SANS BRAS (ARMLESS CARYATID). H20 anonymous engravings.

29 LE PORTEMENT DE CROIX (CARRYING OF THE CROSS). H6. 349×483.
The date at bottom left on a little tablet. The original drawing by Luca Penni is in the Louvre. Dated 1544.

30 PIETÀ. H8. 323×287. Unmarked. The etching is much mixed with engraving. The attribution to Mignon seems convincing. The composition is surely by Luca Penni.

31 CLÉOPÂTRA PIQUÉE PAR UN ASPIC (CLEOPATRA BITTEN BY AN ASP). H11. 425×306. Unmarked. The invention is very likely by Luca Penni. Herbet mentions a drawing of the satyress in the Ecole des Beaux-Arts. The ornamentation was repeated in a print by Master I. ♀. V.

32 ENLÈVEMENT DE PROSERPINE (THE ABDUCTION

OF PROSERPINE). H39 anonymous. 315 × 348.
Date at bottom centre (partly cut off in the reproduced proof). The attribution to Mignon, which Lieure suggests, seems to us entirely convincing. The original drawing by Penni is in the Courtauld Institute, London. Dated 1544.

33 COMBAT D'HOMMES NUS (COMBAT OF NAKED MEN). H68 anonymous. 297-448.
Unmarked. The style is clearly that which is attributed to Jean Mignon. The original drawing by Luca Penni is in the Louvre (Inv. 1401). Herbet believed it was by Perino del Vaga, but mistakenly.

34 VÉNUS AU BAIN SERVIE PAR LES NYMPHES (VENUS BATHING ATTENDED BY NYMPHS). H20. 528 × 430.
Unmarked. The invention seems to us to be by Luca Penni. Note the surprising style of the frame, which seems to reflect an influence of the Flemish ornamenters.

35 MONTANT D'ORNAMENTS (ORNAMENTAL COMPOSITION). H127 anonymous. Oval 300 × 380.
Unmarked. The illegible inscription on the proof reproduced is by hand. The attribution to Mignon suggested at the Bibliothèque Nationale seems to us entirely convincing. The style of these ornaments recalls those of the preceding print.

36 PAYSAGE MARIN DANS UN ENCADREMENT (SEASCAPE IN A FRAME). H117 anonymous. 310 × 418.
Unmarked. The print seems to us certainly executed by Mignon, for the elements of vegetation as well as the figure treatment are characteristic.

37 LA CHUTE DE PHAËTON (THE FALL OF PHAETON). H53 anonymous. 288 diameter.
Unmarked. The attribution proposed by Lieure seems acceptable. The invention is probably by Penni.

38 MARS, VÉNUS ET L'AMOUR (MARS, VENUS AND CUPID). H17. 280 diameter.
Unmarked. There is a second state with accidental marks above the branch at right. The composition may be by Penni.

39 L'ADORATION DES MAGES (ADORATION OF THE MAGI). H3. 309 × 422.
The composition is definitely by Luca Penni.

40-45 These six pieces clearly constitute a suite on the theme of Troy. Luca Penni is the author of the compositions.

40 LE JUGEMENT DE PÂRIS (THE JUDGMENT OF PARIS). H21. 315 × 431.
Unmarked. The original drawing is in the Louvre (Inv. 1395). It is inspired by the composition of Raphael engraved by Marcantonio. There is a smaller (130 × 181) anonymous etching in reverse.

41 L'ENLÈVEMENT D'HÉLÈNE (THE ABDUCTION OF HELEN). H12. 320 × 420.

42 BATAILLE SOUS TROIE (BATTLE BEFORE TROY). H75 of L.D. 328 × 430.
There can be no doubt that this piece is part of the series on the Trojan War, and the style of etching is exactly the same as the other pieces.

43 LE PERFIDE SINON INTRODUIT PAR LES BERGERS DANS LE CAMP DES TROYENS (THE TREACHEROUS SINON BROUGHT INTO THE TROJANS' CAMP BY THE SHEPHERDS). H15. 320 × 448.
The original drawing by Penni is in the Louvre (Inv. 1397) as well as a variant (Inv. 1398).

44 LES TROYENS INTRODUISENT LE CHEVAL DE BOIS DANS LEUR VILLE (THE TROJANS BRING THE WOODEN HORSE INTO THEIR CITY). H14. 320 × 445.
The original drawing by Penni is in the Louvre (Inv. 1399).

45 LE PILLAGE DE TROIE (THE SACK OF TROY). H13. 317 × 435.

46 FEMMES AU BAIN (WOMEN BATHING). H23. 442 × 620.
Unmarked. The composition is certainly by Penni. There is a copy published by N. Nelli at Venice.

47 PRÉSENTATION DE LA VIERGE AU TEMPLE (PRESENTATION OF THE VIRGIN AT THE TEMPLE). H7 anonymous. 349 × 380.
Unmarked. The attribution suggested by Lieure seems acceptable, at the moment when Mignon was closest to L.D.'s style, presumably after the series on Troy. The composition by Giulio Romano is painted in Verona Cathedral.

48 MARCUS CURTIUS SE PRÉCIPITANT DANS UN GOUFFRE (MARCUS CURTIUS PLUNGING INTO A CHASM). H16. 324 × 482.
Unmarked. The composition is most probably by Penni.

49 L'ADORATION DES MAGES (ADORATION OF THE MAGI). H4. 352 × 510.
Unmarked. The composition is without doubt by Penni.

50 SAINT MICHEL COMBATTANT LES ANGES REBELLES (SAINT MICHAEL FIGHTING THE REBELLIOUS ANGELS). H9. 594 × 440.
Unmarked. A drawing of the composition was

attributed to Primaticcio in the Norblin sale, but the invention seems to us certainly by Penni.

51 ENTELLUS ET DARÈS (ENTELLUS AND DARES). H69 anonymous. 309 × 439.
Unmarked. This piece seems to us clearly in the style attributed to Mignon. The composition, whose central motif was inspired by an engraving by Marco di Ravenna, is probably by Penni.

52a LE JUGEMENT DERNIER (THE LAST JUDGMENT). H27. 334 × 450.
Unmarked. The composition may be by Penni. First state.

52b LE JUGEMENT DERNIER (THE LAST JUDGMENT). H27. 425 × 610.
Second state, with the inscription Arrius on the Pope's tiara at right. The impression includes an ornamental frame which Herbet did not know, and which bears various inscriptions.

53 LA MORT D'ADONIS (THE DEATH OF ADONIS). H19. 281 × 240.
Unmarked. There is a second state with the indication 'F.L.D. Ciartes excudit'. The original drawing by Luca Penni, which includes the frame but not the landscape, is in the Teyler Museum, Haarlem.

54 ABRAHAM SACRIFIANT ISAAC (ABRAHAM SAC-RIFICING ISAAC). H39 L.D. 328 × 416.
Unmarked. We do not know how Herbet could have attributed this piece to L.D. since it is characteristic of the style which he himself assigns to Mignon. The attribution of the composition to Primaticcio, which Dimier did not accept, seems to us equally ill-founded. The extensive natural setting is probably the work of Mignon himself.

55a SAINT JEAN PRÊCHANT AU DESERT (SAINT JOHN PREACHING IN THE DESERT). H10. 422 × 590.
Unmarked. The composition is attributed to Luca Penni. Herbet refers to one anonymous copy, and to another on wood published by Nicolas Prevost; there exists another one signed by Giovanni Battista dei Cavallieri.

55b SAINT JOHN PREACHING IN THE DESERT. Detail (landscape and part in stipple).

56 CRÉATION D'ÈVE (THE CREATION OF EVE). H1. 438 × 564.
Unmarked. The composition has always been attributed to Luca Penni.

57 LA TENTATION D'ÈVE (THE TEMPTATION OF EVE). H2. 420 × 560.
Unmarked. The composition is attributed to Penni.

58 ORNAMENT. H106 anonymous. 229 × 324.
Unmarked. It appears to us that this curious asymmetrical ornament resembles that of JM57 in its execution. We cannot say whether Penni invented it.

59a FRAGMENT D'ORNEMENT (FRAGMENT OF AN ORNAMENT). H99 anonymous. 103 × 184.

59b FRAGMENT D'ORNEMENT (FRAGMENT OF AN ORNAMENT). H100 anonymous.
We believe these two fragments are cut from a single print, of which no other proof is known. The style seems like Mignon's.

60 LA MÉTAMORPHOSE D'ACTÉON (THE META-MORPHOSIS OF ACTEON). H22. 430 × 575.
Unmarked. This superb sheet is surely an invention of Penni's, except for the landscape, which is probably Mignon's. Herbet refers to a smaller copy in reverse.

GEOFFROY DUMOÛTIER

Dumoutier's prints, executed in all probability between 1543 and 1547, are difficult to classify chronologically. We have placed at the end four very similar pieces, one of which is dated 1547; these are surely the last. For the rest, which must perhaps be placed, as far as essentials go, close to 1543, we have separated the compositions of several figures from the isolated figures; the uninterrupted suite of the latter best shows a development between the manner of 1543 and that of 1547. No piece is marked or signed in the plate, and those signatures which appear are manuscript (see Introduction). Dumoutier's style is so personal that there are hardly any problems of attribution.

1a and 1b FIN DE LA STÉRILITÉ DE SAINTE ANNE (RD1). NAISSANCE DE LA VIERGE (RD2). (THE END OF SAINT ANNE'S STERILITY. BIRTH OF THE VIRGIN). 156 × 232 together.
These two compositions are etched on the same plate. There is an engraved copy of 1b, which is perhaps by Reverdy (Herbet 25 anonymous engravings).

2 LA VISITATION (THE VISITATION). RD3. 128 × 110.

3 LA NATIVITÉ (THE NATIVITY). RD4. 180 × 128.

4 LA NATIVITÉ (THE NATIVITY). RD5. 243 × 200.

5 LA NATIVITÉ (THE NATIVITY). RD6. 242 × 200.

6   LA NATIVITÉ (THE NATIVITY). RD, XI, p. 84, 1. 147 × 185.

7   LA NATIVITÉ (THE NATIVITY). RD7. 118 × 154.
There is a copy of this piece with variations attributed to Georges Reverdy.

8   JÉSUS PRÊCHANT PARMI LES DISCIPLES (JESUS PREACHING AMONG THE DISCIPLES). RD n.d.; Linzeler 25. 120 × 159.

9   DÉPOSITION DU CORPS DE JÉSUS (THE DEPOSITION). RD, XI, p. 84, 2. 186 × 250.

10   L'ÉVANOUISSEMENT DE LA VIERGE (THE VIRGIN FAINTING). RD8. 116 × 142.
We do not think this is the Virgin's death, as Robert-Dumesnil says, but her fainting at the foot of the Cross.

11   SAINT JEAN DANS L'ÎLE DE PATHMOS (SAINT JOHN ON THE ISLAND OF PATHMOS). RD10. 247 × 162.

12   LA VIERGE COURONNÉE DANS UNE NICHE (THE CROWNED VIRGIN IN A NICHE). RD12. 226 × 126.
The date is on the tablet at right, and on another lower one: 'IEHAN.1.2.' and the French quotation in the margin. Dated 1543.

13   LA VIERGE (THE VIRGIN). RD11. 226 × 126.
On the upright of the niche at right 'I Timo 2' and the French quotation in the margin. An original drawing with some variants is in the Ecole des Beaux-Arts.

14   UNE SAINTE (A FEMALE SAINT). RD13. 222 × 114.

15   SAINT PAUL ASSIS (SAINT PAUL SEATED). RD, XI, p. 84, 3. 230 × 175.

16   UN SAINT ASSIS (A SAINT SEATED). RD, XI, p. 84, 4. 229 × 177.

17   UNE SAINTE ASSISE (A FEMALE SAINT SEATED). RD16. 160 × 120.

18   L'IMMACULÉE CONCEPTION (THE IMMACULATE CONCEPTION). RD9. 160 × 102.
Robert-Dumesnil calls this piece *The Assumption*.

19   LES SAINTES FEMMES ALLANT AU SÉPULCRE (THE SAINTLY WOMEN GOING TO THE SEPULCHRE). RD21. 154 × 114.

20   DEUX HOMMES EN DISCUSSION (TWO MEN IN DISCUSSION). RD22. 162 × 187.

21   SAINT PAUL (?). RD14. 175 × 125.

22   L'ÉGLISE (THE CHURCH) (?). RD15. 187 × 105.

23   ALLÉGORIE (ALLEGORY). RD18. 192 × 100.
Date at centre of the margin. 1547.

24   L'ÉLOQUENCE (ELOQUENCE). RD17. 195 × 108.

25   LA JUSTICE (JUSTICE). RD19. 190 × 100.

26   LA DISCORDE (DISCORD). RD20. 195 × 110.

LÉONARD LIMOSIN

As far as one can judge, all of Léonard Limosin's etchings are of 1544 and in an entirely homogeneous style. All are of religious subjects. We have ranged them in the order of their Biblical reference.

1   L'ANNONCIATION (THE ANNUNCIATION). H1. 250 × 180.
Monogram towards the bottom.

2   LA NATIVITÉ (THE NATIVITY). H2. 257 × 188.
Date and monogram at bottom right.

3   L'ENTRÉE À JERUSALEM (THE ENTRY INTO JERUSALEM). H3. 265 × 185.
The monogram and date at bottom right.

4   LA CÈNE (THE LAST SUPPER). H4. 250 × 185.
Signature and date on a tablet.

5   LE CHRIST AU JARDIN DES OLIVIERS (CHRIST IN THE GARDEN OF OLIVES). H5 and 6 (the same piece). 255 × 190.
Signed and dated.

6   L'ARRESTATION DE JÉSUS-CHRIST (THE ARREST OF CHRIST). H7. 255 × 188. Signed and dated at bottom left.

7   JÉSUS CHRIST RENVOYÉ PAR HÉRODE (CHRIST TURNED AWAY BY HEROD). H n.d. 202 × 185.
Signed at bottom left.

8   LA RESURRECTION (THE RESURRECTION). H8. 261 × 190. Signature and date at bottom right.

THE SUPPOSED JUSTE DE JUSTE

The known etchings by the supposed Juste de Juste must all have been executed in the same period, at a date which cannot be established for lack of evidence, but which, in our view, cannot have been very far from 1543. They form two groups, of which only the first bears the artist's monogram. The attribution of the second group raises no doubts. The series of human pyramids is probably complete in five pieces, for we have come upon three copies constituted in this way.

1 PYRAMIDE DE SIX HOMMES (PYRAMID OF SIX MEN). 280 × 205.

2 PYRAMIDE DE SIX HOMMES (PYRAMID OF SIX MEN). 253 × 204.

3 PYRAMIDE DE SIX HOMMES (PYRAMID OF SIX MEN). 266 × 200.

4 PYRAMIDE DE CINQ HOMMES (PYRAMID OF FIVE MEN). 267 × 205.

5 PYRAMIDE DE CINQ HOMMES (PYRAMID OF FIVE MEN). 270 × 200.

6 FIGURE DE FACE (FRONT FIGURE). 195 × 83.

7 FIGURE DE DOS (BACK FIGURE). 195 × 85.

8 FIGURE DE FACE, TÊTE DE PROFIL À DROITE, BRAS GAUCHE EN HAUT (FRONT FIGURE, HEAD IN RIGHT PROFILE, LEFT ARM RAISED). 194 × 85.

9 FIGURE DE FACE, TÊTE DE PROFIL À GAUCHE (FRONT FIGURE, HEAD IN LEFT PROFILE). 183 × 90.

10 FIGURE DE FACE, TÊTE DE PROFIL À DROITE, BRAS DROITE EN HAUT (FRONT FIGURE, HEAD IN RIGHT PROFILE, RIGHT ARM RAISED). 190 × 86.

11 FIGURE DE FACE PENCHÉE À GAUCHE (FRONT FIGURE LEANING TOWARDS LEFT). 183 × 78.

12 FIGURE APPUYÉE SUR UN BÂTON ET UN SOCLE (FIGURE RESTING ON A STICK AND A PEDESTAL). 190 × 86.

13 FIGURE DE DOS, MAIN GAUCHE RETOURNÉE (BACK FIGURE, RIGHT HAND TURNED IN). 194 × 83.

14 FIGURE DE FACE, BRAS AU-DESSUS DE LA TÊTE (FRONT FIGURE, ARMS ABOVE THE HEAD). 195 × 88.

15 FIGURE DE DOS PENCHÉE À DROITE SUR UN GRAND BÂTON (BACK FIGURE, LEANING TOWARDS RIGHT ON A LARGE STICK). 168 × 87.

16 FIGURE DE DOS AVEC UN GRAND BÂTON (BACK FIGURE WITH A LARGE STICK). 195 × 86.

17 FIGURE DE FACE APPUYÉE SUR UN SOCLE (FRONT FIGURE RESTING ON A PEDESTAL). 176 × 87.

PIERRE MILAN

The pieces which follow are assuredly only a small part of the œuvre whose identification seems to us certain. Moreover, our No. 5, *Jupiter au milieu des olympiens*, is necessarily by Pierre Milan only if one accepts the identification of this artist with Pierre de la Cuffle. Indications concerning the dates of these prints will be found in the Introduction.

1 DANSE DES DRYADES (DANCE OF THE DRYADS). RD74 of Boyvin. 280 × 400.
Inscription at bottom: 'Cum Priuilegio Regis – Quercum erisichtonian dryades cinxere choreis – Rous. Floren. Inuen.' This composition by Rosso is painted in a cartouche below the *Sacrifice* in the Galerie François I. A drawing at the Ecole des Beaux-Arts seems likely to be the preparation for the engraving and therefore probably by Milan. (Kusenberg attributed it to Boyvin, to whom the print was also attributed at the time.)

2 LES PARQUES NUES (THE NAKED FATES). RD31 of Boyvin. 242 × 165.
Unmarked. It is not doubted that the invention is by Rosso. There exist two copies, one anonymous, the other by Sustris.

3 LES PARQUES MASQUÉES (THE FATES WITH MASKS). RD90 of Boyvin. 253 × 416.
Inscription at bottom: 'Rous.de.Rous.Floren.Inuentor:' and at right, 'Cum priuilegio Regis'. This design by Rosso seems to have been intended for some mythological masquerade. A series of masked heads in the same style is also known, and was probably also engraved by Milan (RD78–89).

4 JUPITER ET CALISTO (JUPITER AND CALLISTO). RD73. 180 × 286.
Unmarked. Jupiter, having assumed the appearance of Diana, embraces the nymph Callisto, whom Cupid is about to pierce with his arrow. Dimier showed that this composition is by Primaticcio and was painted in the apartment of the baths.

5 JUPITER AU MILIEU DES OLYMPIENS (JUPITER SURROUNDED BY THE OLYMPIANS). RD33. 490 × 390.

We believe that this piece must be seen as the 'square ceiling' mentioned by Van Mander as the work of Pierre de la Cuffle, who must probably be identified with Pierre Milan. Dimier does not mention this print in his catalogue although Robert-Dumesnil had attributed the composition to Primaticcio, which seems to us entirely justified. But we do not know where this ceiling was located. Robert-Dumesnil reports two states: in the first, only the two top corners were cut, whereas all four are cut in the state reproduced here.

6 CLÉLIE S'ÉCHAPPANT DU CAMP DE PORSENNA (CLELIA ESCAPING FROM PORSENA'S CAMP). RD19 of Boyvin. 400×543.
Inscription at bottom: 'Iulius Romanus Inuentor'. This is one of two plates begun by Pierre Milan and finished by René Boyvin. There exist also an anonymous Fontainebleau etching (Herbet 37) and an Italian chiaroscuro of this beautiful composition. The chiaroscuro bears Maturino's name in place of Giulio's as designer.

7 LA NYMPHE DE FONTAINEBLEAU (THE NYMPH OF FONTAINEBLEAU). RD18 of Boyvin. 305×515. Latin inscription in three lines, and on each side of it: 'Cum priuilegio Regis – Rous. Floren. Inuen.' There is hardly any doubt that this is the 'compartment of Fontainebleau' mentioned by the documents which concern the two engravings of Pierre Milan finished by Boyvin. The ornament is the one in which the *Danaë* of Primaticcio can be seen painted in the Galerie François I (see LD8). Some think that it may be an original project of Rosso's and that Primaticcio substituted his Danae in place of this nymph. The painting one can see today in the Galerie is of the nineteenth century and was painted by Alaux after the print. There exist two old pictures also but they too give the impression of having been painted from the print (Metropolitan Museum, New York, and private collection). It is interesting that the inscription alludes to a sculpture and not a painting. There is an anonymous copy published by Valesio in Venice.

7 *Detail* THE NYMPH OF FONTAINEBLEAU.

DOMENICO DEL BARBIERE

The catalogue of Domenico del Barbiere proposed by Herbet includes twenty-seven numbers, whereas we reproduce only twenty-five plates in all, while adding a new piece (DB1). Two pieces with monogram, *La Sainte Famille* (H10), and *La Madeleine pénitente* (H11) have not been found, as well as a *Femme debout* (H27, unsigned and of doubtful attribution), even though Herbet reports it in the Bibliothèque Nationale. *Dix hommes nus dans des rochers* (H13) seems to us in a style different from Domenico's. Finally, Herbet attributes two etchings, *La Renommée* (H14) and *Pandore* (H15, subject identified by Panofsky), which bear the monogram D.B. Nowhere else did Domenico use this monogram, and no other etchings by him are known. Besides, we see no resemblance of style between these pieces and the work of Domenico. Certain indications make us think that these etchings are from northern Italy rather than Fontainebleau; it is not impossible that they are by the same hand as the landscape etchings signed D.B., which are attributed to Dirk Barentsen, but we cannot confirm this. Since it has not been possible for us to suggest even a tentative chronological order for the work of Domenico del Barbiere, we have arranged the plates according to subject.

1 LA VIERGE À L'ENFANT (VIRGIN AND CHILD). H18 anonymous. 188×116.
Unmarked. This piece which Herbet classifies among the anonymous etchings is in fact entirely engraved with the burin. The freedom of the cut, the superb draughtsmanship, the presence of corrections – very rare in burin engraving – make us believe that this engraving may be the work of Domenico del Barbiere. But it is not without hesitation that we attribute it to him, for all the other pieces which we retain in his œuvre are signed. The only known proof is in poor condition and cropped, so it may have lost a monogram.

2 LE MARTYRE DE SAINT ÉTIENNE (THE MARTYRDOM OF SAINT STEPHEN). H1. 272×155.

Signature at bottom left. The coat of arms on the saint's chest are those of the Dintevilles. The print may reflect some painting executed for a member of this family, either by Domenico or by Primaticcio, who worked for the Bishop of Auxerre, François Dinteville. The composition is an adaptation of the one Giulio Romano painted for the Church of St Stephen in Genoa.

3 GROUPE TIRÉ DU JUGEMENT DERNIER DE MICHEL-ANGE (GROUP FROM MICHELANGELO'S LAST JUDGMENT). H2. 364×220.
Signed at bottom left. The inscription at the top indicates the origin of the subject. It does not seem that this section of the *Last Judgment* was copied from another engraving (it differs from those we know

in the way it is cut out and the groups are placed). Could this reflect an extract taken by Primaticcio or Domenico himself?

4 ANGES PORTANT LES INSTRUMENTS DE LA PASSION (ANGELS CARRYING THE INSTRUMENTS OF THE PASSION), from Michelangelo's *Last Judgment*. H3. Arched 193 × 391.
Signature at bottom right, and inscription at left explaining the origin of the subject. It is the lunette at the top left of the *Judgment*.

5 MARS, VÉNUS ET L'AMOUR (MARS, VENUS AND CUPID). H5. 67 × 108.
Monogram at bottom centre. Herbet thinks the invention is by Rosso, but we believe it may be by Domenico himself.

6 AMPHIARAUS. H4. 324 × 229.
Signature at bottom left and title of subject at top. The figure is a famous magician, one of the Argonauts. Heinecken attributed the composition to Primaticcio, and Bartsch to Rosso. Herbet makes no comment, but Kusenberg accepts it as Rosso. Perhaps Domenico invented it himself, as the style seems to us somewhat different from Rosso's.

7 LE BANQUET D'ALEXANDRE LE GRAND (THE BANQUET OF ALEXANDER THE GREAT). H6. 247 × 364.
Signed at bottom left, with the inscription towards the right: 'A.FONTANA. BELO BOL'. Herbet recorded a first state without the inscription, but we have not encountered a proof of it. The composition by Primaticcio, whose original drawing is in the Louvre, was painted in the chamber of Madame d'Etampes.

8 CLÉOPÂTRE (CLEOPATRA). H12. 262 × 120.
Monogram on the chest (or sarcophagus). This lovely print may have been composed by the engraver himself.

9 LA GLOIRE (GLORY). H7. 283 × 220.
Signed with complete name at bottom right; the title GLORIA at top left. There is a second later state with the indication 'P. Mariette ex.'. The invention is by Rosso if, as is generally believed, this is one of the two figures which framed the bust of François I above the door of the small room, replaced in the nineteenth century by the *Nymphe de Fontainebleau* by Alaux.

10 SQUELETTES ET ÉCORCHÉS (SKELETONS AND ÉCORCHÉS). H8. 236 × 334.
Signature at bottom left. It is thought that this plate reflects a book on anatomy which, according to Vasari, was planned by Rosso. But it may be that the composition as it is here represents an adaptation by Domenico of several drawings by Rosso.

11 PAYSAGE DANS UN ENCADREMENT ORNEMENTAL (LANDSCAPE IN AN ORNAMENTAL FRAME). H9. 175 × 182.
Monogram at top left. This print, with its very Rosso-like spirit, may have been invented by Domenico. It is not an etching, as Bartsch (followed by Herbet) affirms, but a burin engraving.

12–22 SUITE D'ORNEMENTS (SUITE OF ORNAMENTS).
We have not been able to find a complete copy of this series. In describing it, Herbet confused Domenico's originals with an etched copy of them in reverse; he called them a second state of the plates because they are numbered and the originals are not. Renouvier attributed the copy to Ducerceau, probably justly. The copied series, which does not include the introductory piece, is not only in reverse but also offers a variant – two motifs of plate 2 are eliminated and used in plate 3, of which no original is known. This makes us wonder whether the etched plates for which we have no engraved correspondents are in fact from originals by Domenico, or whether they were additions made by Ducerceau. Hence we include here the etchings which lack prototypes, but without being certain that originals by Domenico existed. These ornaments, in the style called 'grotesque' because of their antique origin in the 'grottoes' of the Palatine in Rome, are of an exquisite invention. Numerous *pentimenti* attest the freedom of the printmaker. In the introductory piece, the 'grotesques' are difficult to relate to the central subject which emerges from the typical ornamental vocabulary of Fontainebleau.

12 PIÈCE LIMINAIRE (INTRODUCTORY PIECE). H16. 130 × 197.
Signature at top centre.

13 PREMIÈRE PLANCHE (FIRST PLATE). H17. 130 × 190.

14 SECONDE PLANCHE (SECOND PLATE). H18. 130 × 190.

15 TROISIÈME PLANCHE (THIRD PLATE), etching attributed to Ducerceau. H19. 130 × 190.

16 QUATRIÈME PLANCHE (FOURTH PLATE), etching attributed to Ducerceau. H20. 130 × 190.

17 CINQUIÈME PLANCHE (FIFTH PLATE). H21. 130 × 195.

18 SIXIÈME PLANCHE (SIXTH PLATE). H22. 130 × 193.

19 SEPTIÈME PLANCHE (SEVENTH PLATE), etching attributed to Ducerceau. H23. 130 × 190.

20 HUITIÈME PLANCHE (EIGHTH PLATE). H24. 128 × 192.

21 NEUVIÈME PLANCHE (NINTH PLATE). H25. 127 × 193.

22 DIXIEME PLANCHE (TENTH PLATE). H26. 126 × 190.